MONOGAMY IS A MYTH

Craig Michael Lewis

Dedication

To my beloved family,

This book is dedicated to each of you whose unwavering love, guidance, and support have shaped me into who I am today.

To my **mother**, whose boundless love and nurturing spirit have been my anchor through life's storms, thank you for showing me the true meaning of love.

To my **father**, your strength, wisdom, and example of integrity have taught me invaluable lessons about being a man.

To my **sister**, your endless patience, understanding, and companionship have been a constant source of comfort and inspiration.

To my **cousin**, your boldness, resilience, and courage have shown me that fearlessness is the key to unlocking our fullest potential.

Together, you have each contributed a piece to the puzzle of my existence, shaping my beliefs, values, and aspirations.

This book is a tribute to your profound impact on my life, and I am forever grateful for your presence on this journey.

With deepest love and gratitude,

Craig Michael Lewis

About the Author

Greetings, Dear Reader.

Allow me to introduce myself. My name is Craig Michael Lewis, and I hail from a humble town nestled just outside the bustling city of Houston.

After bidding farewell to the halls of high school, I found my calling in the air conditioning trade. I honed my skills working on residential properties for years, gradually mastering the craft until an opportunity arose in 2006 when I joined the union. From there, my journey led me to commercial properties, where I applied my expertise with dedication and passion.

In 2020, a new chapter unfolded as I embarked on a different kind of venture – writing. With a desire to explore the depths of human experience and share my insights with the world, I delved into literature, embarking on several projects that have since become a labor of love.

Beyond my pursuits in the professional realm, I am blessed with a loving family. I am the proud father of two sons, and I have the privilege of sharing this journey with a supportive brother and two wonderful sisters who have been pillars of strength and inspiration throughout my life.

As I invite you to journey through the "Monogamy is a Myth" pages, I extend my heartfelt gratitude for your curiosity and willingness to explore new ideas. May this book spark thought-provoking conversations and ignite a flame of introspection within you.

With warm regards,

Craig Michael Lewis

Preface

Welcome to *"**Monogamy is a Myth**."* Before you delve into the pages of this book, I want to express the essence of its purpose and the journey it invites you to embark upon.

This book is an exploration, a journey of self-discovery, and a challenge to conventional thinking. Here, I share my thoughts, ideas, and perspectives on the concept of monogamy, but I do so with the utmost respect for differing viewpoints. My aim is not to persuade you to adopt my beliefs or to convince you that your way of thinking is wrong. Instead, I invite you to consider alternative perspectives, question societal norms, and examine your beliefs with an open mind.

Throughout these pages, I delve into the complexities of relationships, love, and the human heart. I ask probing questions about the nature of monogamy, challenging assumptions and inviting you to reflect on what aligns with your desires and values. Is monogamy innate to human nature, or is it a construct imposed by society? What role does societal pressure play in our choices regarding relationships? And most importantly, what does your heart truly desire?

This book is not a definitive answer to these questions. Instead, it catalyzes introspection, sparking conversations and prompting readers to reevaluate their beliefs and choices. It covers many topics surrounding monogamy, from its historical and cultural roots to its implications for modern relationships. Above all, it encourages you to listen to your inner voice, to honor your truths, and to embrace the richness of diversity in the human experience.

As you journey through the following chapters, I urge you to approach the material with an open heart and mind. Engage in dialogue, challenge assumptions, and dare to explore the depths of your convictions. Through such exploration, we can only truly uncover what brings us fulfillment and authenticity in matters of the heart.

Thank you for joining me on this journey.

Craig Michael Lewis

Contents

Chapter 1: Myth Buster

Alright, folks, let's dive headfirst into the whirlpool of modern dating and its ever-twisting dynamics. Someone out there once dropped a real gem – wait 90 days before you get down and dirty with someone new. Yeah, you heard that right—ninety whole days, like some emotional layaway plan.

And who could forget the classic words of the one and only Fred Sanford? "You Big Dummy!"

Now, let's chew on this a bit. This 90-day rule has been echoing through the corridors of dating advice like a mantra from love gurus. It's like this cultural relic we've dusted off and slapped a modern label on. But let's be real here – in this world of instant gratification, where swiping right is the new courtship, this rule seems almost archaic, doesn't it?

And then there's Fred, with his no-nonsense, cut-to-the-chase humor. Imagine you're lost in life's wilderness, your heart famished for affection. Suddenly, this 90-day-old honeybun of a rule appears seemingly the sweetest thing in the world. But once you're back in the bustling city of love, will you rummage through the trash for a half-eaten relationship or head straight to the store for something fresh?

Why endure 90 days of emotional starvation when the feast or famine could be figured out in a single day?

It's a gamble, sure, but in the casino of love, aren't all bets off?

So, let's ask ourselves: Is this 90-day rule a timeless love strategy or just an outdated game plan in the modern world of romance?

Now, let's shimmy down the timeline and unravel the historical tapestry of this infamous 90-day rule in dating culture. Back in the day, when courtship was a high-stakes game played in the salons and parlors, this rule might've been the secret playbook. But how did this relic of romantic strategy shimmy its way into our modern love lives?

One minute, you're strolling through the pages of history, and the next, this rule is splashed across every self-help book and relationship blog. This rule transformed from an old-world whisper to a prime-time strategy thanks to media moguls and literature maestros.

You've seen it, right?

Those sappy rom-coms where the clock's ticking down on the love bomb, all wrapped up in a neat, 90-day package.

But let's chew on the societal snack this rule serves up. It's like society's brand of relationship seasoning sprinkled over the meaty reality of our love lives. This rule whispers sweet nothings about patience and virtue, but then there's the gritty truth of our swipe-right, instant-match world. It's a cultural tug-of-war between the slow-burn romance of yesteryears and today's fast-forward love stories.

So, as we peel back the layers of this 90-day onion, we're left with teary eyes and a question – is this rule a timeless token of love and wisdom or just a cultural fad, dressed up in the fancy pants of tradition? Where does this antiquated artifact stand in the grand bazaar of dating advice?

Roll up your sleeves, folks, because now we're diving into the deep end of the psychological pool behind this whole 90-day no-romp rule. Let's face it – the human mind is a tricky beast, especially when it comes to matters of the heart and, well, other areas.

So, why do the love doctors prescribe this 90-day waiting period? It's all about the tease, the anticipation, the slow burn of delayed gratification. Picture this: you're on a roller coaster of emotions, climbing up, up, up for 90 days, the anticipation building with every tick of the clock. It's like waiting for that final season of your favorite show – the wait might drive you nuts, but it also makes the payoff oh-so-sweet.

But here's the twist – this whole waiting game isn't just about playing hard to get or following some antiquated rule. It's a psychological tango. Waiting can crank up the emotional intimacy, turning what could be a quick fling into something deeper. It's like cooking a gourmet meal instead of microwaving a frozen dinner – it takes longer, but the taste?

Unbeatable.

Yet, let's not ignore the flip side. This wait can be a double-edged sword. All that anticipation, all those built-up expectations – they can skyrocket, creating a fantasy that reality can't match. It's like exciting a movie in your head for months, only to walk out of the theater and say, "Eh, it was alright."

So, as we wade through the murky waters of the 90-day rule, we gotta ask – is this psychological strategy a recipe for true love or just a surefire way to set ourselves up for a letdown? Only time, and maybe a bit of heart, will tell.

Let's shuffle the deck and lay out a hand where the 90-day rule and spontaneity face off. It's like choosing between a meticulously planned gourmet meal and a wild, midnight snack raid – both satisfying but so different.

On one side, you've got the 90-day rule, the slow cooker of romance. It's like marinating your relationship with anticipation, mystery, and emotional connection.

The benefits?

You're building something that could be more than a flash in the pan. It's about savoring each moment, each conversation, adding layers of depth that instant gratification can't touch.

But hold up, let's not forget the thrill-seekers, the spontaneity squad. These folks would jump out of a plane first and then check if they have a parachute. For them, love is in the now, the electric spark of the unexpected. The benefits? It's raw, it's real, and it's packed with adrenaline. No waiting, no wondering – just pure, unfiltered connection.

However, every rose has its thorn. The 90-day rule can sometimes turn that sizzle into a fizzle, expectations piling up like a tower ready to topple. And spontaneity? Well, it can be a firework that fizzles out just as fast, leaving you wondering what in the world just happened.

So, what's the real deal?

Take Gary and Tina.

They went the 90-day route, and guess what?

They built a bond that was more than skin deep. But then there's Mike and Elisa, who threw caution to the wind and dived right in – and they're still riding that wave. The moral of the story?

Whether you're a planner or a pantser, it's all about playing your cards right in the game of love.

Let's slice into this honeybun metaphor and see what sweet, gooey insights we can find about the economics of dating and relationships. This 90-day rule? It's like a market strategy for your love life, where the currency is time and the investment is emotional.

Think about it – in economics, it's all about supply and demand, right?

Apply that to dating, and this 90-day rule becomes a scarcity tactic. It's like telling someone they can't have that last piece of cake in the fridge. The more they can't have it, the more they want it. So, when you play by this 90-day rule, you're not just playing hard to get – you're upping your value in the dating stock market.

But here's the kicker – just like that 90-day-old honeybun, the longer something's off the market, the more its perceived value skyrockets. It's like holding onto a vintage wine, hoping it'll age into something exquisite. The wait and the anticipation all add to the allure and desirability. That's the power of scarcity in action.

Yet, just like any economic model, there's a flip side.

What happens when the market crashes? When the buildup doesn't live up to the hype? Suddenly, that honeybun you've fantasized about for 90 days tastes like any other pastry. It's a risky game – balancing the scales of desire and expectation, all while trying to hit that sweet spot in the economics of love. So, as we mull over this honeybun of a dilemma, we gotta ask – is playing the market really the way to win in the game of love, or are we just setting ourselves up for a sugar crash?

Now, let's swing the spotlight onto some real talk – personal stories and interviews about this whole 90-day shebang. It's like opening a box of assorted chocolates; you never know what you'll get.

First up, meet Jenna. She played by the 90-day rule like it was gospel. She said it was like holding a winning lottery ticket, waiting for the draw.

The result? A relationship that bloomed like a slow-cooking stew, rich and satisfying. Jenna's takeaway? Patience is a virtue that can pay off in emotional dividends.

But then, there's Carlos. He chucked the rulebook out the window. For him, waiting was like sitting on a ticking time bomb. He went with his gut, and guess what? He found a connection so electric it could light up a city block. His lesson? Sometimes, the best things in life are unplanned.

And let's not forget Lisa, who tried the 90-day wait but found herself in a plot twist. The buildup was epic, but the climax?

A letdown like a deflated balloon at a birthday party.

Her insight?

Sometimes, the fantasy is better than the reality.

So, what's the moral of these tales?

It's like picking your path in a choose-your-own-adventure book. Whether you're a slow-burn believer or a spontaneous soul, the journey of love is a personal script.

The 90-day rule?

It's just one of the many scenes you might play out. Ultimately, every heart writes its own story, rulebook or not.

Now, let's roll out the red carpet and shine a spotlight on the glitzy world of media and celebrity influence in the dating game, specifically the Steve Harvey rule. When someone like Steve Harvey – a big shot with a megaphone to the world – lays down a rule like the 90-day wait, it echoes across the dating landscape like a love guru's chant.

It's not just Steve, though. Turn on the TV, flip through a magazine, or scroll through your feed, and you'll see celebs and influencers dishing out advice like they're serving up a Thanksgiving feast. Their words become the gospel for many starry-eyed romantics, looking to these stars as their North Star in navigating the choppy waters of love.

But let's put on our critical thinking caps and dissect this Steve Harvey rule, shall we?

In a world where swiping right is the new courtship dance, does playing the waiting game fit the bill? It's like trying to read a map from the 90s in the age of GPS – quaint but maybe a bit out of touch.

Sure, the rule's got its perks – building anticipation, deepening emotional connections, all that jazz. But in an era where authenticity and instant connections are the new norm, this 90-

day rule can feel like a relic from a bygone era, like waiting for a dial-up connection in the age of high-speed internet.

So, as we tune into this episode of 'Love in the Time of Influencers,' we're left wondering – is this rule a one-size-fits-all, or is modern love a more customized fit tailored to each individual's heart? In the celeb-studded sky of relationship advice, maybe it's about finding the star that shines brightest for you.

Let's wade into the murky waters of ethics and morality in the dating scene, mainly focusing on this 90-day rule. It's like stepping into a philosophical boxing ring, where personal freedom and societal norms are the heavyweight contenders.

Let's break it down. Imposing a rule like the 90-day wait – isn't that a bit like putting a leash on love?

It's a tangle of ethics where the line between guidance and control gets blurry. On one hand, this rule is paraded like a banner of self-respect and caution. It's like saying, "Hold your horses; let's not dive headfirst into the deep end without checking for sharks."

But then, flip the coin, and you're staring at personal freedom, winking back at you. It's about owning your choices and desires, unshackled by the chains of do's and don'ts. In the grand theater of love, shouldn't every act be unscripted, driven by the heart's whims?

Now, let's talk morals. In the dating game, decisions about intimacy are more than just physical. They're moral choices stitched with threads of values, beliefs, and personal boundaries. The 90-day rule, in this light, is like a moral compass handed down by society. But here's the kicker – not everyone's north points in the same direction.

So, as we juggle these ethical balls and moral dilemmas, the question looms – is the 90-day rule a guiding star or a moral maze?

In the dance of love and desire, is it the rhythm we follow, or do we make up the steps as we go along?

Like love itself, the answer is a riddle wrapped in a mystery.

Let's take this 90-day rule on a world tour and see how different cultures weigh in on this wait-before-you-date debate. It's like flipping through a global dating manual, each page having a different take on love's waiting game.

In some corners of the world, the 90-day rule would get you a blank stare – it's like telling a fish to wait 90 days before swimming. Take, for example, countries steeped in traditional values where relationships often follow a more measured, gradual path. Here, the 90-day rule isn't just a suggestion; it's a sprint compared to their marathon of courtship rituals. It's about family, honor, and long-term commitments, woven into the fabric of their dating culture like a well-stitched tapestry.

Then you jet off to the more liberal societies, where the 90-day rule might seem like a relic from an old romance novel. Love's more of a freestyle dance than a choreographed ballet in these parts. It's about connection, chemistry, and the here and now. Waiting for 90 days? That's like putting a timer on your heart and expecting it not to beat out of rhythm.

But let's not just globetrot; let's also time-travel. How does this rule square up against the changing tides of love and relationships through the ages?

In the grand romance timeline, the 90-day rule is like a snapshot in a constantly evolving album. What was once the norm becomes the exception, and vice versa. It's a dance of values, norms, and desires, changing to the rhythm of societal and cultural beats.

So, as we wrap up this introduction, let's take a step back and look at the big picture. We've talked about history, psychology, economics, and personal stories. We've shone a light on the celebrities and dissected the morals and ethics of it all. And let's not forget our trip around the world, peeking into love's many windows.

As we set the stage for the rest of this love saga, remember – this book is not just about whether you should wait 90 days. It's about understanding love's intricate layers, from the whispers of history to the shouts of modernity. It's about seeing love as a feeling and a journey through time, culture, and self.

So, dear readers, buckle up. We're just getting started on this rollercoaster ride through the amusement park of love, relationships, and everything in between. Let's explore, question, and maybe even break some rules. After all, aren't the rules made to be rewritten in the world of love?

Diving into the psychology behind relationship anticipation, we embark on a journey through the twisted corridors of the human mind, where desire and expectation dance a sultry tango. Picture this: you're in the throes of a fresh romance, and every tick of the clock pumps adrenaline straight into your heart. You've got this 90-day countdown etched in your mind, each day a teasing whisper, a promise of ecstasy.

Now, think about those nights, long and heavy with desire. You're lying there, alone, your mind a playground for fantasies. It's like having a treasure chest, but you've lost the key, and all you can do is imagine the riches inside. The thought alone fuels your longing and turns mundane moments into a simmering pot of anticipation. It's not just about the physical act; it's about the build-up, the mental striptease that goes on day after day.

The psychology behind this isn't just about sex; it's about the human craving for emotional rollercoasters. We're wired for the chase, the hunt. We get a kick out of the yearning, the not-having. It's like being on a diet and dreaming about that forbidden chocolate cake. The longer you wait, the sweeter it seems.

But here's the kicker — this waiting game isn't just butterflies and roses. It's a mental battlefield. You start second-guessing and overthinking.

What if the wait isn't worth it?

What if the fantasy is better than the reality?

It's like buying a ticket for the greatest show on Earth, only to worry whether it'll live up to the hype.

In this 90-day saga, you're not just counting days but riding an emotional tsunami. It's a mix of fear, excitement, doubt, and hope. You're emotionally investing in this countdown, each day a deposit into your bank of desires. And all this time, your brain's cooking up a storm, a delicious cocktail of hormones and emotions.

This wait becomes a character in your relationship's story. It's the unsung hero, villain, and sidekick rolled into one. It turns your romance into a ticking time bomb of passion, where every conversation and every touch is laced with unspoken promises and unfulfilled desires.

In this game of anticipation, the rules are unwritten, and the outcomes are uncertain. It's a psychological thriller, with you and your partner as the lead characters. Will the wait forge a stronger bond, or will it crumble under the weight of its own expectations? Only time will tell. But one thing's for sure – this isn't just about waiting for sex. It's about the exhilarating, maddening, and utterly human experience of wanting something so bad that every fiber of your being is on edge. Welcome to the 90-day wait, where the mind plays the most compelling game of all.

Now, let's switch gears and roll into the aftermath of this heart-thumping, pulse-racing 90-day journey – the impact of potential disappointment. It's like reaching the final chapter of a gripping novel only to find the last pages torn out. Those three months of fiery anticipation, fantasies, and dreams can crash down with the weight of a lead balloon when reality doesn't measure up to the mental hype.

Picture this: you've spent 90 nights riding the waves of your imagination, each fantasy more vivid than the last. You've built a cathedral of desire in your mind, every detail a testament to your longing. But then, the moment arrives, like walking into a mirage. The touch, the feel, the ecstasy you envisioned echoes in an empty hall of disappointment. It's the gourmet meal that turns out to be just bland soup.

This plunge from the peaks of anticipation to the valleys of disappointment isn't just a mood killer; it's a psychological gut punch. You've been riding high on dopamine, the brain's brand of pleasure drug, only to crash into the harsh ground of reality. It's like being promised a Ferrari and ending up with a toy car. The emotional whiplash can leave you reeling, questioning your judgment, choices, and feelings.

This fallout can be a twisted tangle of frustration, regret, and even a sense of betrayal. You've invested emotionally, mentally, and, let's not forget, physically, into this countdown to ecstasy. And when the payoff is a dud, it's not just a letdown; it feels like a breach of an unspoken contract.

And let's talk about the ghost of this disappointment – it doesn't just pack its bags and leave. Oh no, it lingers, casting a long shadow over your relationship. Every touch, every kiss becomes tinged with the memory of that anticlimax. It's like a stain on your favorite dress that just won't come out, a reminder of what could have been but wasn't.

In the end, this journey of anticipation and its potential crash landing is more than just a waiting game. It's a psychological expedition where the risks are high, and the falls can be steep. It's a gamble where the jackpot is a dream come true, and the consolation prize is a lesson learned the hard way. So, as you navigate this tricky terrain of love and longing, remember – the 90-day rule is not just a countdown; it's a tightrope walk over the chasm of human emotion. And when you play with fire, sometimes you end up with more than just warmth; you get burned.

Strap in 'cause we're about to take a wild ride around the globe, checking out how different corners of the world view the whole dating scene, especially when stacked up against our notorious 90-day rule. Let's just say not everyone's playing the same game.

First stop, let's hit the West. Here, dating's like a fast-food joint – quick, convenient, and you've got plenty of options on the menu. The 90-day rule? For some, it's like a fancy, three-course meal in a world of drive-thrus. Sure, some folks like to savor the anticipation and build a connection, but let's be real – many are just swiping their way to the next best thing. The rule in these parts?

It's more of a suggestion, and often, it's tossed out the window after a couple of good dates and a few flirty texts.

Now, zoom over to more traditional societies. Picture this: places where relationships are a slow-burn, more about long-term commitments than quick flings. Here, the 90-day rule isn't a challenge; it's child's play. They're looking at a timeline that's more like months, even years, where dating is a family affair, and every move is weighed against cultural expectations and traditions. In these parts, patience isn't just a virtue; it's the whole damn script.

But wait, there's more. Let's talk about those places where arranged marriages still rule the roost. Here, dating as we know it isn't even on the table. It's like comparing apples and, well, dinosaurs. The whole idea of waiting 90 days to hit the sheets?

Outrageous because the sheets are often reserved for the post-wedding extravaganza.

And let's not forget the romantics, the ones who still pen love letters, wait for that one true love. For them, the 90-day rule is like a badge of honor. They're not just waiting for sex; they're waiting for that fairytale, sweep-you-off-your-feet romance. It's a different ballgame – one where every second of waiting adds to the grandeur of the love story.

On the flip side, you've got the rebels, the rule-breakers. For them, the 90-day rule is a joke, a relic of a prudish past. They're all about living in the moment, following their hearts (or other parts), no matter where it leads them. The thrill of the chase, the rush of a new romance – that's their drug, and they're not about to put a timer on it.

So, what's the deal with the 90-day rule?

It depends on who you ask and where you're standing. It's a mixed bag of cultural norms, personal beliefs, and societal expectations. It's like we're all dancing to the beat of our drums, and while some are in it for the slow, rhythmic sway, others are all about the fast-paced, heart-thumping rave.

It all comes down to this – dating, love, the whole relationship shebang, is as diverse as the world we live in. Whether waiting 90 days or diving right in, it's your call. Remember, there's no one-size-fits-all in this wild world of love and dating. So, pick your path, make your rules, and let the heart lead the way.

Alright, let's talk about the raw, untamed side of us humans – the biological drives in sexual behavior. It's like a primal beat that thumps in the depths of our being, urging us to merge, mingle, and get down and dirty. This ain't just a whimsical dance of romance; it's the nitty-gritty of nature, the call of the wild that's been drummed into us since the dawn of time.

In the grand circus of life, sex isn't just a show; it's the main event. It's that primal urge, the itch you just gotta scratch. And why? Because deep down, in the murky waters of our DNA, we're wired to procreate, to keep the human race hustling and bustling. It's not just about pleasure; it's about survival, baby.

Think about it. When you're hot for someone, it's not just your heart talking; it's your hormones. Testosterone, estrogen, and pheromones are nature's potent cocktail. It's like your body's got its agenda, and when the chemistry's right, boom — you're hooked, lined, and sunk into the sea of desire.

Don't think it's all just animal instincts. This biological drive has got style and finesse. It's the reason you appreciate her curves, her scent, the way she laughs. And ladies, it's why you're drawn to his strength, swagger, and smile. We're programmed to seek out the best mate, the alpha in the pack, to ensure our genes are passed down in style.

Now, let's circle back to our friend, the 90-day rule. In this modern dating jungle, waiting 90 days is like holding back a tidal wave. You're fighting against millions of years of evolutionary programming. Your body's screaming, "Let's get it on," but society's whispering, "Hold your horses." It's a clash of the titans, a battle between our civilized selves and wild, untamed desires.

And let's not sugarcoat it — this waiting game can be a real bitch. It's like having a feast laid out in front of you, but you can't touch it. Your whole being is hardwired to dive in, but nope, you've got to sit on your hands and wait. It's frustrating, it's challenging, and man, does it test your resolve.

But here's the kicker – even with all this biological programming, we ain't just slaves to our desires. We've got something that sets us apart from the rest of the animal kingdom – our big, beautiful brains. We can think, we can choose, and we can control these urges. Or at least, we try to. It's what makes the whole dance of dating and mating such a thrilling, frustrating, mind-boggling adventure.

So, there you have it. Our sexual behavior isn't just a whim or a fancy; it's a deep-rooted, biological siren song. It's the eternal tango between our animal instincts and our human sensibilities. And whether you choose to wait those 90 days or dive right in, just remember – you're playing the oldest game in the book, the game of life, love, and the pursuit of that oh-so-sweet ecstasy.

Let's get down and dirty with the evolutionary backstory of our human mating practices and tie in that spicy bit about polygamy from our previous analysis. It's time to understand why, from an evolutionary standpoint, humans have been mixing it up, from monogamy to polygamy and everything in between.

Let's start with the basics.

Evolution's all about the survival of the fittest, right? And in the grand scheme of things, it's not just about surviving; it's about passing your genes to the next generation. That's where our sex drive comes into play, a powerful force pushing us to mate and keep the human race going.

Now, think about polygamy. It's been around since, well, almost forever. It's not just a random cultural fluke; there's a reason behind it. For men, spreading their seed far and wide means a better chance of their genes surviving and thriving. It's like playing the lottery – the more tickets you buy, the better your chances of hitting the jackpot. And in this case, the jackpot is a bunch of little ones carrying your DNA into the future.

But it's not just about quantity; it's about quality, too. Conversely, women are wired to look for the best possible mate, someone who can provide and protect, ensuring their offspring have the best shot at life. It's like quality control for the gene pool.

This tug-of-war between different mating strategies has been shaping human behavior for millennia. It's why some men, deep down, feel this urge to conquer, to spread their wild oats far and wide. And it's also why women can be picky, always looking for the right partner who brings the right stuff to the table.

But hold up, it's not just a free-for-all. Humans are complex creatures. We've got emotions, societal rules, and all sorts of complications that muddle up these primal urges. That's why we see such a smorgasbord of relationship styles across different cultures and eras. From strict monogamy to open relationships and polygamy, we're trying to balance these evolutionary urges with the realities of modern life.

Let's face it, though – no matter how much society changes, those deep-rooted instincts aren't going anywhere. They're a part of who we are, hardwired into our brains and bodies. That's why, even in a world of dating apps and 90-day rules, we still feel that primal pull, that urge to connect, to mate, to keep the human story going.

So, the next time you're wrestling with the dating game's do's and don'ts, remember – behind all the romance, the flirting, and the heartbreak, there's a primal beat, an evolutionary drum that's been driving us since the dawn of time. Whether waiting 90 days or jumping right in, we're all just trying to navigate this wild ride called love, driven by forces as old as life itself.

Alright, let's dive into the deep end of gender-specific expectations in the wild world of sexual encounters. We're talking about a realm where men and women play by different rules, driven by age-old instincts and societal scripts.

Let's cut to the chase: men are often seen as the conquerors, the hunters. It's not just a stereotype; it's woven into their very fabric. From the crack of dawn, their biology is shouting, "Go forth and conquer!" It's like they're hardwired for the chase, their eyes on the prize, and let's be real, the prize often isn't just an emotional connection – it's sex.

This isn't just some macho bravado; it's evolutionary coding. Back in the caveman days, spreading their genes was the name of the game, and it seems like old habits die hard. This translates to men often being more inclined to jump the gun, not too keen on playing the waiting game.

The 90-day rule?

For many guys, it's like sitting on a ticking time bomb while their primal urges are doing the countdown.

On the flip side, women have historically been the gatekeepers, the choosers. Sure, they've got their fiery desires, but they're often playing a longer game. They're wired to sift through the noise, to find that diamond in the rough. For many women, waiting 90 days is more than just a rule; it's a test, a way to weed out the fleeting flings from the potential real deals.

But let's not paint everyone with the same brush. We're living in a world where these lines are getting blurred. Women are embracing their sexuality more openly, and men are learning that there's more to relationships than just the physical rush. Yet, despite this modern twist, those old-school scripts still lurk in the background, whispering the old ways.

This clash of expectations can lead to all sorts of fireworks and fiascos. Like when a guy's all revved up, ready to go, but the lady's putting on the brakes, not because she's not into it, but because she's playing the long game. Or when a woman's ready to dive deep, the guy's just skimming the surface. It's a dance as old as time, each step loaded with unspoken expectations and ancient rules.

And let's talk about disappointments and letdowns when the wait doesn't quite live up to the hype. Ladies waiting for Mr. Right might find Mr. Right Now falling short, leaving them wondering if the wait was worth it. And the gents, after counting down those 90 days, might find themselves in an anticlimactic showdown, their conquest not quite the epic saga they'd imagined.

So, there you have it — a battlefield where gender expectations and biological urges collide, where ancient scripts play out in modern bedrooms. It's a game of cat and mouse, a tango of desire and restraint, each side navigating the minefield of sexual politics, trying to find that sweet spot where the wait, the chase, and the catch-all come together in perfect harmony.

In the entangled world of relationships, cultural and societal influences play a crucial role in shaping gender roles, particularly in the context of sexual encounters. The expectations and norms dictated by society often lead to a dichotomy in how men and women approach relationships and sex, as vividly illustrated in our excerpt.

Let's dissect this complex dance of gender roles, starting with the men, those often viewed as the natural conquerors. It's in their DNA, right? From morning wood to the deep-seated urge to spread their genes, men are often portrayed and perceive themselves as hunters in the realm of romance and sex.

This isn't just some macho trope; it's a narrative steeped in history and biology, where men have been the aggressors, the pursuers of sexual conquest. The morning wood is not just a bodily function; it symbolizes this primal urge, a daily reminder of their innate desires.

Now, flip the script, and you have women, traditionally cast in the role of the choosers, the gatekeepers of sexual encounters. They are often expected to be more discerning, to wait, to evaluate. This dynamic suggests a deeper, more emotional approach to sex and relationships, where physical intimacy isn't just about the act itself but about what it represents — connection, stability, and, sometimes, a strategic move in the complex game of love.

The bedwarming example in our excerpt isn't just a throwaway line. It's a nod to historical gender roles where women were seen as passive recipients of male desire, an expectation that's been challenged and redefined over time but still lingers in certain corners of our collective psyche.

But here's where it gets interesting. As traditional as they may seem, these roles are not set in stone. They're evolving, shifting with the tides of societal change. Today, women are increasingly taking the reins, owning their sexuality and desires more openly. And men are learning that there's more to relationships than conquest, that emotional depth and connection are as vital as the physical act itself.

This evolution, however, doesn't erase the ingrained scripts passed down through generations. It creates a complex landscape where old norms clash with new realities, where the dance of seduction and romance is as much about navigating these expectations as it is about personal desires.

In a world where women can wait and men supposedly can't, where men are conquerors by nature, and the most effortless conquest is deemed to be sexual, the real challenge lies in balancing these age-old narratives with the quest for genuine, fulfilling relationships. It's about recognizing these influences, understanding their origins, and deciding how or if they fit into our personal tales of love and desire.

So, as we traverse this tricky terrain, let's remember that our roles in the saga of love aren't just about biology or tradition. They're about choice, breaking molds, and sometimes, rewriting the scripts we've been handed. It's a journey of self-discovery, where the end goal isn't just to fulfill societal expectations and find a connection that resonates with our deepest, most authentic selves.

In the tantalizing tango of sexual relationships, anticipation is a key player, casting a spell of excitement and, often, unexpected twists. It's a psychological rollercoaster, especially when we consider the characters in our excerpt, each brimming with desires, expectations, and the inevitable dance with disappointment.

Let's crack open the psychology of this anticipation. Imagine you're in the game, the 90-day countdown is on, and every passing day amps up the excitement. It's like a kettle simmering on the stove, each day turning up the heat. The mind becomes an artist, painting vivid pictures of what's to come, each stroke fueled by longing and fantasy.

For our characters, these three months are more than just a wait; they're a build-up of intense, almost tangible sexual energy. The thoughts, dreams, and even solo acts are all part of this anticipation. It's not just physical; it's an emotional and mental crescendo, with each passing day adding to the symphony.

But here's the catch: with great anticipation often comes the risk of great disappointment. The human mind is a master storyteller; sometimes, the stories it weaves are too good to be true. When the moment of truth finally arrives, reality might fall flat compared to the elaborate fantasies. It's like craving a gourmet meal for months, only to be served a fast-food burger.

This psychological effect can be profound. The higher the anticipation, the steeper the fall into disappointment. The reality can be a harsh wake-up call for our characters, who've spent nights fantasizing about the perfect encounter. The disappointment isn't just about the physical act; it's about the shattering of a carefully constructed fantasy, a dream that took 90 days to build.

The anticipation also plays tricks with their perception. It magnifies every detail, every touch, every kiss, setting an almost unattainable standard for reality to match. It's a psychological trap where the line between fantasy and reality blurs, leaving them grappling with unmet expectations.

But let's not forget that anticipation has its upsides, too. It can heighten the sense of connection, making the eventual coming together more intense and passionate. It's a double-edged sword, where the potential for an extraordinary emotional and physical connection balances the risk of disappointment.

The psychological effects of anticipation in sexual relationships are a complex mix of excitement, fantasy, risk, and, sometimes, disillusionment. For our characters and many in the real world, the journey of anticipation is as crucial as the destination. It's about enjoying the build-up, savoring the wait, and learning to navigate the tricky waters of expectations versus reality. Because sometimes, the best parts of the story are the chapters leading up to the climax.

In the heated aftermath of sexual disappointment, the mind becomes a battleground of emotions and thoughts, a stark contrast to the fervent anticipation that once filled every waking moment. For ninety long days, they'd been riding a wave of excitement, imaginations running wild with every possible scenario, each more enticing than the last. But what happens when reality falls painfully short of these vivid daydreams?

The letdown, it's like a gut punch. After all the build-up, the fantasies, the late-night longing, the endgame feels like a cruel joke. It's not just the physical dissatisfaction; it's the crumbling of a meticulously constructed castle in the sky. The heart and the mind don't just feel let down; they feel betrayed as if those ninety days were a deceitful promise of something that was never meant to be.

And then there's the self-doubt.

Was it me? Were my expectations too high? This isn't just about hurt pride; it's a deep, gnawing question that eats away self-confidence. Every moment of excitement, every fantasy now feels like a foolish gamble that didn't pay off, leaving nothing but a void of regret and what-ifs.

The impact of this disappointment isn't fleeting; it lingers, casting a long shadow over what once seemed like a clear path to fulfillment. Suddenly, every future prospect is tinged with skepticism. The mind, once so sure of what it wanted, now hesitates, scarred by the memory of that letdown. It's a psychological barrier, a wall built brick by brick with every dashed hope and unmet expectation.

And amid this turmoil, the thought looms large: "Never again."

It's a vow, a defense mechanism against future heartache. The ninety-day rule, once a beacon of hope, now feels like a fool's errand, a path they swear never to tread again. It's a retreat, a step back into the safety of lowered expectations, where the risk of disappointment is minimized, but so is the chance of true fulfillment.

The psychological aftermath of sexual disappointment is a complex web of hurt, confusion, and self-protection. It's a journey from the heights of anticipation to the depths of disillusionment. This path leaves its travelers wary but wiser, their fantasies now tempered by the harsh lessons of reality.

Let's cut through the noise and get real about communication in the bedroom and beyond. It's not just pillow talk; it's about being brutally honest with what you want, expect, and what's going through your head. Think about it – you're both keyed up for three months, building castles in the air, dreaming about what it will be like. But what if you're not on the same page? That's where straight talk comes in.

Picture this: you've been counting down those 90 days, and your mind's running wild with all sorts of scenarios. But hey, what if you're imagining a fireworks show, and your partner's thinking of a cozy campfire?

That's a mismatch waiting to happen. That's why it is vital to lay it out raw and unfiltered. You gotta talk about what turns you on, what doesn't, and everything in between—no beating around the bush.

And it's not just about sex. It's about what you're looking for in this whole dance of romance. Are you in it for the long haul or just a quick tango? Mixed signals can lead to some serious crash and burn. Ain't nobody got time for that!

Now, imagine the aftermath of a letdown. You're there, wondering why things went south, why the earth didn't move under your feet. That's when you wish you'd had that straight-up conversation earlier. Maybe one of you wanted something more adventurous, or perhaps some signals got lost in translation. Whatever it is, not talking about it only makes the confusion worse.

So, here's the deal: whether it's before you jump into bed or after things didn't quite go as planned, you gotta talk it out. It's like fixing the leaks before the ship sinks. You both deserve to know where you stand without any guesswork.

This communication thing – it's not just a nice-to-have; it's a must-have. It's what separates a sizzling affair from a damp squib. You gotta put your cards on the table. It might be awkward, but it's a hundred times better than fumbling in the dark, hoping you're doing it right.

In a nutshell, clear communication is the secret sauce to keeping things hot and real. It's about being bold enough to say what you want and smart enough to listen to what they want. So, next time you find yourself counting down those 90 days, make sure you're talking as much as you're fantasizing. Trust me, it'll save you a world of confusion and help you hit the jackpot or at least know where you stand. No more guessing games, just straight-up real talk. That's how you play the game of love and lust, winning style.

Let's talk brass tacks about what happens when the wires get crossed and expectations crash and burn in the bedroom. It's about the afterburn of those 90 days – the days you spend in a heady mix of daydreams and wild fantasies, only to crash into a pit of disappointment. It's like expecting a gourmet feast and ending up with a bag of stale chips.

You see, it's all about the hype, the buildup. You're locked in this dance, circling around what's to come, but when D-day hits, it's like someone popped your balloon with a rusty needle.

All that waiting, the ticking clock, it's supposed to lead to fireworks, right?

But what if it fizzles out?

That's where things get really messy, real fast.

Picture this: you've been marking off days on your calendar, your mind spinning tales hotter than a summer blockbuster. But then the main event rolls around, and it's like showing up at the circus only to find the clowns have gone home. It's not just the letdown that gnaws at you. It's the feeling of being duped like you've been sold a ticket to a blockbuster that turns out to be a B-grade flick.

Now, you're left with a truckload of 'what ifs' and 'whys.' Like, why didn't it pan out like in your dreams? Was it just a case of bad chemistry, or did you oversell the fantasy in your head? This ain't just a scratch on your ego; it's like questioning the whole script you've written in your mind.

And let's not forget the fallout. It's not just about picking up your bruised heart and moving on. It's like every time you try to get back in the game, that ghost of disappointment whispers in your ear, reminding you of the flop show you just witnessed. It's a shadow that trails you, coloring your every move, every new possibility with a tint of doubt.

But here's the kicker — this mess of miscommunication and unmet expectations it's not just a personal sob story. It's a loud wake-up call to the fact that in this game of hearts and bedsheets, assuming you're both reading from the same page is the fastest way to write a tragic end to your love story.

So, what's the takeaway from this crash course in bedroom blunders? It's simple — talk it out, lay it bare. Because when it comes to the tango of sheets and hearts, flying blind is for the birds. It's about matching your script with theirs, so when the final act comes, you're both stars of the same show, not extras in different movies.

It's all about getting real with what you want, what they want, and finding that sweet spot where expectations meet reality. Otherwise, you're just actors in a play where everyone forgot their lines, stumbling around the stage hoping for a miracle. And let's be honest, who wants to watch that show?

Being the optimist that you are, you decided that his poor dick game isn't the end-all. There may be hope in his fellatio game. Then he literally bites you! He was eating your pussy as you had asked him to.

At that point, you say, "That's it!!! Game over! Fuck Steve Harvey and his 90-day rule! Neva again!!"

Think about it for a second. You've been talking and hanging out with the person. Discovering what things they like, their favorite foods, movies, and television shows. Finding out what their passions and goals are. During this time, you also form a daily pattern with this person. From regular morning text to cuddle time on the weekends. By doing this, you both are learning from each other and gradually getting into the other's system, even though in the back of your mind, you're thinking about sex.

The more you talk and hang out, the more intense every moment becomes. That's why when the time does come for you to have sex, you feel as though it's the best sex you've ever had. That is, if there are no sexual derailments such as the ones we've mentioned. If the sex is no good, then the relationship is going nowhere. Waiting 90 days is a waste of time, and it can cause you to waste more time by creating a false sense of satisfaction because, after 90 days, you have become locked in.

Robert Beck, also known as Iceberg Slim, said, "An emotional debt is hard to square."

So, here's the thing: this whole waiting game is like a bad hand in poker - you're just sitting there, hoping for a win, but deep down, you know the odds are stacked against you. It's like the world's been spinning this yarn, telling us that if we wait and play by these arbitrary rules, everything will be sunshine and rainbows. But let's not kid ourselves; life ain't a fairytale.

This whole 90-day rule, it's a trap, a setup. It's like you're cooking a stew, simmering it for hours, hoping for that perfect flavor. But when you finally take a bite, sometimes it's just bland. And you're left wondering, "What the hell was I waiting for?" It's a bitter pill, realizing that all that waiting and anticipation was for nothing.

We've been fed this idea that monogamy, waiting, and playing by the rules is the path to happiness. But let's face it, not everyone's cut out for that. Some folks are more like free birds, not meant to be caged. They're out there, craving variety, new experiences, something that stirs the blood. And who's to say that's wrong?

The truth is, we're all wired differently. For some, the idea of one partner for life is like a dream come true. But for others, it's like a straitjacket, squeezing the life out of them. We're talking about desires, the raw, primal stuff that stirs deep within. It's like trying to tame a wild beast – it might play along for a while, but its true nature always comes out.

Now, I'm not saying throw all caution to the wind. But maybe, just maybe, it's time to rethink the whole one-size-fits-all approach to relationships. Perhaps it's time to accept that for some of us, the open road, the chance to explore and experience more than one, is what really gets our engines running.

So, next time you're sitting there, following some made-up rule, ask yourself, "Is this really me?"

Maybe you're the kind who thrives in the open field, not in a walled garden. And if that's the case, embrace it. Life's too short to be living someone else's version of happiness. It's all about finding your way and path to fulfillment. Because in the end, that's what counts – being true to yourself, your desires, and your nature.

In Narcotics Anonymous, they preach that falling back into old habits after being clean amplifies the addiction. Now, ain't that a thought? Apply that to sex, treating it like the drug it can be, and suddenly, those 90 days of abstinence are like a dry spell before a storm. The idea is that once you hit day 91, everything becomes more intense, more passionate – the best damn sex you've ever had. Both of you, hooked on each other like never before. That sounds like a dream, right?

But here's the kicker – this whole 90-day rule? It's like a chess game, and let's not kid ourselves. It's usually the woman moving the pieces. It's not that they're all about manipulation; it's just that most men don't give a damn about waiting. The truth is, very few guys are down for this game. It goes against their nature. Men, by their very essence, are conquerors, seekers of new territories, always on the prowl. And top of the conquest list? You guessed it, pussy.

Let's break it down further. Think about the everyday man – who wakes up with a hard-on. What's he supposed to do? Lay there and wait for it to pass? Hell no. He's wired to plunge into something warm, something welcoming. It's a primal, basic instinct. This whole scenario screams one thing – men are not naturally monogamous. They're hunters, gatherers, not settlers.

Now, this ain't about bashing monogamy or putting polygamy on a pedestal. But let's face it; the history of mankind is littered with tales of men with harems and multiple partners spreading their seed like they're trying to populate a new planet. It's in the scriptures and in the history books. Ever wonder why there's no commandment against having more than one partner? That's because, at the core, men are programmed for variety, for the chase.

So, where does this leave us with the 90-day rule? It's like putting a lion on a vegetarian diet – unnatural and downright cruel. This rule is a modern-day invention, a societal construct designed to tame the wild. But can you really tame a beast? Can you suppress millions of years of evolutionary wiring with a self-help book and a promise of a fairy-tale ending?

Let's be real – this rule is more about control, about steering the relationship in a certain direction. And while we're at it, let's smash another myth – the notion that men need time to figure out if a woman is 'the one.' Bullshit. Men know, often instantly, if a woman is a keeper. They don't need three months to figure it out. If they're into you, they're into you. Period.

The world keeps spinning these tales of happily ever after, of the prince and the princess locked in eternal monogamy. But look around – the world is changing. People are exploring, questioning the norms, and breaking the chains. The idea of one person for life is becoming just that – an idea, not a rule.

Maybe it's time to rethink these rules, these societal norms that we cling to. Maybe it's time to accept that the open road is more appealing than the fenced yard for some. That doesn't make it wrong. It just makes it different. And in a world as diverse and complex as ours, differences should be celebrated, not condemned. Because in the end, what matters is not how many you're with but the joy and fulfillment you find in those connections. That's the real deal. That's what counts.

Is it really just a fluke that a man wakes up with his flag at full mast every morning? Nah, it's nature calling, loud and clear. This ain't just some morning routine; it's a primal urge as old as time itself. What's a man supposed to do, ignore it? That's like telling the sun not to rise. He's going to find his way to a soft, warm embrace, the kind only a woman can provide. That's the real deal, the raw truth of it. It's a dance as old as humanity itself.

My old man used to say, "Son, it's a fool's game trying to tether a man to just one woman."

Ain't that the truth? Men roaming the Earth have always had a wandering eye and a restless heart. You look back through the annals of history, and it's there, clear as day – men spreading their love far and wide. Polygamy wasn't just accepted; it was the norm, the way of life. It's in every culture and every religion. The Bible's chock-full of fellas with more than one missus. Nowhere does it say, "Thou shalt not enjoy the company of multiple ladies."

Now, think about this – monogamy, this whole one-man-one-woman jazz, it's a relatively new fad. It's like someone decided to rewrite the rules without asking the players. For thousands of years, men lived in a world where loving more than one woman wasn't just okay; it was expected and respected even. Then comes this new age philosophy trying to box men into this one-size-fits-all relationship model. Who decided that? Why's the world so hell-bent on selling this dream of monogamous bliss?

Let's get something straight – a man's nature ain't something you can just flip like a switch.

Do you think centuries of evolutionary hardwiring can be undone with a couple of self-help books and some societal pressure? Come on now. Men are built to roam, to seek, to conquer. That's not just some macho bullshit; it's biology, it's psychology, it's the raw, unfiltered essence of manhood.

Do you ever notice how society's always shoving this monogamy narrative down our throats? Like it's the only way, the righteous path. But here's the kicker – it ain't working. Look around, man. Divorce rates are sky-high, affairs are as common as colds, and folks are more confused about love than ever before. Maybe, just maybe, it's because we're all trying to live a lie, to fit into a mold that doesn't quite fit.

Now, I ain't saying polygamy is the answer for everyone. But I am saying that maybe it's time we stop pretending there's only one way to love, one way to live. Maybe it's time we accept that for some, loving more than one ain't a sin or a shame; it's just their truth, their reality. And maybe, just maybe, if we embrace that, we might find a little more happiness and truth in our lives.

It's about finding what works for you, what makes you whole, what sets your soul on fire. Suppose that's one person, great. If it's more, that's great too. The point is love ain't a one-size-fits-all deal. It's a wild, wonderful spectrum; we must all find our place without judgment or fear. That's the real journey and adventure. And who knows, maybe along the way, we'll find that what we've been taught isn't necessarily true for us. Maybe we'll find our way, our own path to happiness. And maybe, just maybe, that's what it's all about.

Let's roll the dice and ask ourselves a simple question: who threw the first orgy? Man or woman? I'd bet my last dollar it was a man. This ain't just a wild guess; it's rooted in the very nature of men. We're talking about creatures who don't just think about sex. They live and breathe it. Every waking moment, there's that primal urge gnawing at them.

Now, let's get real for a second. This whole 90-day rule? It's a farce, a circus act. Think about it. Do you really believe the average Joe is sitting around, counting the days on his fingers, waiting to jump into bed? That's a laugh. Men are simple creatures in this complex dance of love and lust. They see what they want, and they go after it. No calendars are needed, and no alarms are set. It's all about the here and now.

But here's where it gets twisted. Society's got this skewed image of what a man should be and should do. Everywhere you look, there's this bombardment of sex – it's in the music blaring from our speakers, the movies flashing on our screens, even in the way people dress to step out for groceries. It's like the world's this giant, walking, talking temptation. And yet, the same society that flaunts sex in our faces is the one preaching patience, monogamy, and this ridiculous 90-day waiting game.

Let's cut through the crap for a second. Even if a man decides to play by these rules and commit to one woman, it's like he's fighting his own nature. It's an internal battle between what he's wired to do and what society expects him to do. And for what? To fit into some cookie-cutter image of a 'good man'?

Please...!

And here's another kicker – the idea that a man needs three whole months to figure out if a woman's the one for him? That's rich. Men aren't wired to overthink love and attraction. It's not a Rubik's cube; it's more like a gut feeling, an instinct. If he knows, he knows. No need for a trial period.

But, oh boy, let's talk about the man who coined this 90-day rule – Steve Harvey. I can't help but wonder if he was just throwing a bone out there, maybe a secret message to his daughter or something. Because, let's face it, the whole concept reeks of a TV show plot, not real life.

Back to the point – men and their natural inclinations. Since dawn, men haven't been programmed for this one-woman show. Look at history, at the tales of kings and warriors. It's a saga of men spreading their love and seed far and wide. It's not just about lust; it's about legacy, about imprinting themselves on the fabric of time.

So, when we talk about men, sex, and relationships, let's not kid ourselves. The whole monogamy spiel? That's a square peg in a round hole situation. Men are as much victims of this societal construct as anyone else. They're pushed into this mold, told to suppress their very nature to fit into a narrative sold to us as the 'right way.'

At the end of the day, whether it's the first orgy thrower or the modern man, the story remains the same. Men are told to battle their instincts and walk a line arbitrarily drawn in the sand. And for what? To chase a dream that might not even be theirs. It's about time we started questioning these norms and rules and asking ourselves: Are we living our truth or just playing parts in a script we didn't write?

Let's dive into the deep end of this conversation, starting with the cold, hard truth about women and their, let's say, 'equipment malfunctions.' You ever find yourself with a lady, all hyped up, only to discover she's got a situation down there that's like solving a damn geometry problem? Yeah, that's a tough break, like navigating a maze with no exit. It's like every thrust sends you into a black hole of disappointment. And when it's broken, it's broken. There ain't no mechanic shop for that sort of repair.

Now, let's chew on this for a sec – even a bombshell like Halle Berry, who's got men drooling over her left, right, and center, has whispers floating around about her skills, or lack thereof, in bed. Sure, she's got this aura, this shimmer that makes guys wanna treat her like she's made of glass, all delicate and precious. But think about it – has anyone ever really seen her getting down and dirty, getting her hair messed up, and being taken for the wild ride she deserves? Nah, in the real world, it's all smoke and mirrors. You see her in Monster's Ball with Billy Bob Thornton, and it's like a finely choreographed dance, nothing like the raw, untamed passion that leaves you breathless.

Let's cut to the chase here. We're dealing with the grand illusion of perfection, the fantasy that some women are these untouchable goddesses, so pure and pristine that they can't be anything but perfect in every way. But here's the kicker – they're human, just like the rest of us. They have flaws and quirks; sometimes, their equipment isn't up to the task.

Now, this isn't about bashing women or anything. It's about peeling back the layers of fantasy we've been fed our whole lives. It's about understanding that real life ain't a Hollywood movie. There's no script or director yelling 'cut' when things get too real. And when it comes to sex, well, it's as real as it gets.

Here's where the whole monogamy debate comes into play. We've been sold this dream of finding 'the one' – that perfect match who'll fulfill every desire, every need. But let's face the facts: life ain't a fairy tale. People come with their own set of issues; sometimes, what you see isn't what you get.

You might end up with someone as exciting in bed as a sack of potatoes, and what then?

Stick around because society says you gotta be monogamous?

Hell no. This is where the whole concept of open polygamy starts making a whole lot of sense. Why limit yourself to one flavor when you can have the whole damn buffet?

It's about variety, about experiencing everything life has to offer. It's about understanding that it's okay to want more, to explore, and not be confined by outdated notions of what a relationship should look like.

It's about being true to yourself, about not settling for mediocrity in the sack or anywhere else in life. It's about breaking free from the chains of monogamy and embracing the wild, unpredictable ride that is polygamy. So, next time you find yourself stuck with a broken vagina or a partner who just doesn't do it for you, remember – there's a whole world out there waiting for you. Go out and conquer it, just like nature intended.

Taking a leaf out of Eddie Murphy's stand-up act RAW, you get the real picture. The man's got it right – once you hit the sweet spot and make a woman holler that "ooowee," you're holding the keys to the kingdom. Picture this: you're at home, cozy with someone who isn't your main squeeze. She walks in, eyes wide, and you just hit her with the old 'you're dreaming' line. Like magic, she's back to bed, no questions asked. You might even throw in a sandwich request, and she's on it like white on rice. That's the power of the "ooowee."

Let's talk about Lisa Raye and Halle Berry. Lisa's spilling the beans on Halle, saying she ain't all that in the sack. Now, Lisa's a veteran in the game of "ooowee." At 55, she's still killing it, but in pussy years, she's a ripe 46 – perks of being a redbone, I guess. I don't make the rules, but light-skinned women have always had this sort of grace.

Then there's Karlie Redd, 49 but a solid 76 in pussy years. She's been around the block, but don't let that fool you. She's got what we call 'the snapper' – a pussy so good, it does all the work. Imagine just laying there, and she's pulling you in, milking you without you having to do a damn thing. Karlie's the type to get any man she wants – old, young, hitched, or on his way to the slammer. She's unstoppable.

Now, what does all this tell us? It's a clear signal that monogamy ain't all it's cracked up to be. Why stick to one flavor when there's a whole buffet out there? This ain't just about getting your rocks off; it's about experiencing variety and living life to the fullest. It's about knowing you don't have to be shackled by society's outdated rules.

Think about it – we're living in a world where guys like Eddie Murphy and women like Lisa Raye and Karlie Redd are showing us the ropes. They're telling us, in not so many words, that the traditional path ain't the only one. These folks are living their best lives, sampling everything on the menu, and who are we to say they're wrong?

It's about time we start looking at relationships through a new lens. Why settle for one when you can have many? Why limit yourself when the world is full of diverse, exciting experiences? Monogamy might work for some, but for the rest of us, polygamy is where it's at.

It's all about choice. If monogamy is your jam, go for it. But if you feel like you're missing out, maybe it's time to explore. I mean... why limit yourself?

Remember, life's too short to stick to one flavor. So, go out there, find your "ooowee," and see where it takes you. Just like Eddie, Lisa, and Karlie, you might find that polygamy is your true calling.

In wrapping up this opening chapter, we've dipped our toes into a world that challenges the conventional. It's been a journey through the tales of Eddie, Lisa, Karlie, and others – a glimpse into lives outside the monogamous box. These stories aren't just idle gossip; they're signposts pointing towards a different path, one less traveled but rich in its offerings.

As we turn the page, leaving behind this first chapter, we realize there's more to relationships than the age-old narrative of monogamy. It's a world brimming with possibilities, where the rules aren't set in stone, and personal choice reigns supreme.

So, as we step into the next chapter, let's keep an open mind. Let's explore these alternative paths with curiosity and see where they lead us. Maybe, just maybe, we'll find that the unconventional is more suited to our nature than we ever imagined. With that thought, we move forward, ready to delve deeper into the intriguing world of relationships, where every turn is a discovery and every story a lesson in the vast tapestry of human connection.

Chapter 2: Nature and Man

Man has always believed that he is the smartest creature on the planet, even though he can't seem to figure out nature. And because he cannot figure nature out (as in his customary chauvinistic behavior), he calls it mother nature because of its high winds, tornados, hurricanes, tsunamis, and earthquakes.

Alright, let's cut to the chase. This chapter isn't here to sugarcoat anything. It's about throwing a hard, cold look at monogamy and seeing how it stacks up against what we find in nature and the anthropological record. The truth? It's a bit of a mess.

First off, let's talk about nature. Here's the thing: you hardly see strict monogamy in the animal kingdom. Sure, you've got your swans, bald eagles, penguins, and a few others, but they're more like the exceptions that prove the rule. Most animals are out there living their best lives, not sticking to just one partner. It's like a free-for-all out there – if nature's a party, monogamy is definitely not getting the invite.

Now, switch gears to humans.

Throughout history, various cultures have practiced polygamy. It's been the norm in many societies. Look at the kings and emperors of the past – those guys weren't exactly poster children for monogamy. And it's not just ancient history. Even today, you'll find communities where polygamy is alive and well. But here's the kicker: in the grand scheme of things, the concept of sticking to one partner for life is relatively new and, dare I say, a bit unnatural.

Let's not forget the big elephant in the room – cheating. It's like the universe's way of giving us a reality check. No matter how many vows are exchanged, the stats on infidelity are pretty telling. It's almost like a part of us rebels against the idea of monogamy. It's a tough pill to swallow, but it's there.

So, what does all this mean?

Well, it's not a free pass to break hearts left, right, and center. But it does raise some questions.

Like, are we trying to fit a square peg into a round hole with this whole monogamy thing?

Are we fighting our nature, or is it just a case of society's expectations messing with our heads?

I'm not here to give you the answers. But I am here to make you think. Maybe it's time to reevaluate what we consider 'normal' regarding relationships. Maybe it's time to accept that there's no one-size-fits-all approach to love and sex. After all, if nature's taught us anything, it's that diversity is the spice of life.

So, there you have it - a no-nonsense, straight-talking look at monogamy versus the natural and anthropological findings. It's a bit of a wild ride, but hey, that's what this chapter is all about. It makes you think, question, and maybe, just maybe, make you see things a little differently.

Those who believe and practice monogamy go against what comes naturally to each of us. Man is supposed to be fruitful and multiply. Monogamy is a learned behavior and practice.

Polygamy should be a way of life for us all.

Right after we drop the bombshell that monogamy might be going against our natural instincts, it's crucial to understand why this conversation matters in the grand landscape of human relationships. Let's get real here: we're not living in some fairy tale where everyone's happily ever after involves the same story.

This isn't a one-size-fits-all situation.

Let's think about it.

We're constantly bombarded with this idea that finding 'the one' and sticking to it for life is the ultimate goal. But what if that's just a made-up rule?

What if we're all forcing ourselves into a mold that doesn't fit?

This discussion isn't just academic; it's about how we live, love, and relate to each other.

Take a look around.

How many people do you know who are truly, deeply satisfied with monogamy?

And I mean genuinely satisfied, not just putting up a front for the' gram or because society says that's how it should be.

Then, on the flip side, how many people are out there feeling trapped, unfulfilled, or even dishonest because monogamy just isn't their jam?

This isn't about giving people a free pass to cheat or hurt others. No, it's about questioning whether we've been fed a one-track narrative and ignoring the vast array of human experiences and desires. Monogamy works for some, and that's cool.

But for others?

Maybe not so much. And that's cool, too.

Acknowledging and discussing these differences is crucial. It's about understanding and accepting the diversity in human relationships. It's about recognizing that what works for one person might not work for another. And most importantly, it's about creating a world where people can be honest with themselves and each other about what they truly want and need in relationships.

By challenging the monogamy narrative, we're not just stirring the pot for the sake of it. We're opening the door to more honest, fulfilling relationships. Whether that's monogamy, polygamy, or anything else on the spectrum of human connection, it's about finding what truly works for you.

And that, my friends, is a discussion worth having.

Question for thought.

Why was there no mention of animals getting killed during the last great tornado or any great disaster for that fact?

Because they are smarter than humans, they know when danger is coming and get out of the way.

Is this because they are smarter, or are they in tune with nature and instinctively feel and sense the signs of danger?

Have humanoids become so detached from nature that they cannot tap into this intuition that every earthly creature has?

It's just like that voice that tells us not to go around the corner because danger is lurking.

Is that voice the same voice that alerts animals of dangerous weather on the horizon and to prepare to flee?

Religions such as Islam and Hinduism, as well as some Christian communities such as Mormons, believe and practice polygamy, and it seems to work for them. For the discussion of this book, the focus will be the American Christian culture we reference as the base of conversation.

Now, pertaining to the laws of nature, those who feel it is not natural for one man to be with one woman argue that all animals/species mate instinctively at will.

When speaking about monogamy or mating for life, we must acknowledge some high level of loyalty there. An animal's loyalty is love to the death, figuratively and literally. It will be loyal to its mate; if domesticated, it will be loyal to its owner.

For example, a dog will do anything for its owner by protecting its owner from anything and anybody. If a burglar breaks into your home, all you have to say is "Get him" and it's on and poppin' in that burglar's life.

You won't ever have to worry about that burglar again. But if that burglar had come with a bitch in heat, the situation would have a different outcome.

The situation would be something like this.

The burglar kicks your door wide open and gets dead on your ass while your own four-legged best friend charges past you to get to a bitch. You're on your own. Just like Dr. No Nutts wrote in her book *A Bitch in Heat is King*.

In her book, she says that a dog in heat is her day to rule because all the male dogs are after her, and she can make them do whatever she wants. Remember that the dog is not one of the animals known to be with one mate unless it has been domesticated and is forced into monogamy.

Alright, diving back into the thick of it – this whole monogamy versus polygamy thing isn't just some academic chin-wagging; we're slicing through layers of biology and anthropology here. Let's keep it real and to the point.

Biologically, it's like humans are decked out for diversity.

Think about animals and their mating dances; they're not exactly the poster children for monogamy, are they?

That's nature's own algorithm working its magic – mixing and matching genes to keep the species robust and kicking. Humans, for all our tech and threads, are still part of this wild kingdom. Deep down, beneath all the social constructs, an animal instinct doesn't always sing the tune of *one partner for life.*

Now, let's swivel to the anthropological viewpoint, which is a snazzy way of saying we're checking out human behavior from the perspective of culture and history. This is where the plot thickens. Roll back the tape of human history, and you'll see a smorgasbord of relationship models.

Maybe we need to go back to a time when life was so much easier, back to caveman times. I'm not saying let's go around clubbing women across the head. But they say if it's not broke don't fix it.

I'd like to tell you a story.

Once upon a time, there was a caveman by the name of Aug who was the smartest man in the village, and because of this, he ran his village. A caveman by the name of Boo came along, and he was six feet tall and three hundred pounds – you get the picture right? He was just a beast in size.

Aug had the finest and prettiest girl in the village by the name of Mu. Boo wanted her for himself, so he clubbed Aug over the head and took Mu for his own.

Mu loved Aug, but what could she do?

Every night after Boo would finish having his way with her, he'd pass out. Mu would sneak off into the night to Aug. This continued for months until Aug couldn't take being without Mu anymore.

So he devised a plan.

He set out to find some shells from hatched dinosaur eggs. The shells were known to be very sharp. He found several pieces, including one two feet round in size. He took the shells back to the village, dug a hole, and placed the pieces of shells inside.

After he covered the hole with bamboo leaves, he went looking for Boo. When he found Boo, he taunted him and ran toward the hole. Boo chased him, and he fell into the hole. The shells cut Boo's leg so badly that he bled out.

That was the world's first Boo bee trap.

Nature can be funny, but embracing it can be pretty pleasurable.

Even till a few hundred years ago, polygamy was as standard as morning coffee. From kings and chiefs to the everyday Tom,

Dick, and Harry (or Jill, Jane, and Joan), multiple partners were part of the deal. We're talking about alliances, power plays, and resource sharing, and sometimes, it was just about good old carnal desire.

Now take Alexander 'AE' Edwards (natureposeuse- a heterosexual male who is in tune with nature but might have multiple women to fulfill his desire), for example, who is Amber Rose's ex-boyfriend. He has gotten caught cheating with at least twelve women during his relationship with her. This behavior is a pattern. Usually, if a person gets caught over three times, whether drug dealing, burglary, or pickpocketing, you need a different process, but in his case, I believe it's a cry for help.

He doesn't know how to express himself to Amber. How does he tell the woman he loves and who loves him back that he was not honest with her from the very beginning and that he sold her dreams of the ideal socially accepted monogamous relationship because he knew that she would not understand his desire to be with various women even though he loves her. When Amber saw all the text communications between him and those twelve women, he was defeated by his desires.

He's not going to change because he is at peace with himself. She must embrace his love for her and either get on board or move on. But she will never find a man to love her like he does.

Now that being Megan thee Stallion, the finest female on the planet who is young, successful, talented, and rich.

What more could any man want in a woman?

Guys would kill to be with her. Now, with all that going on, her man will be cheating on her before his book is published. Once again, he loves her with all his heart.

Ladies, I know what you're saying. He's a damn fool. As so many women have in this situation, Megan will likely ask herself, *"Why? Am I not enough? What do I need to do?"*

The answer is "Nothing."

It goes back to the bread dildo. You gave him your bread stick one too many times. It's just nature. Don't blame yourself.

Diving deeper into the religious aspect, busting some myths is essential. Regarding relationships, religion is often seen as a monolith of monogamy. But that's not the whole picture. It's time to zoom in and get a clearer view.

Let's start with Christianity. It's a big umbrella, right?

Underneath, there are many denominations and interpretations of scripture. While mainstream branches like Catholicism and many Protestant denominations advocate monogamy, there are other Christian groups where polygamy isn't just tolerated; it's part of the fabric.

Take, for instance, certain fundamentalist sects that have roots in Mormonism. They've embraced a version of Christianity where polygamy is a crucial component. It's not about flouting the rules; for them, it's about following a different interpretation of religious teachings.

Moving over to Islam, polygamy is more openly discussed and practiced. The Quran allows a Muslim man to marry up to four wives, provided he can treat them all fairly and equally. It's not about indulgence but responsibility and equitable treatment within the bounds of faith.

Hinduism, with its vast array of practices and beliefs, also has historical roots in polygamy. While modern Hindu society primarily practices monogamy, the religious epics and scriptures like the Mahabharata and Ramayana are replete with kings and gods practicing polygamy, illustrating its acceptance in the past.

In a nutshell, the relationship matrix within the context of religion is far more nuanced than a simple black-and-white, monogamy-only picture.

Different faiths and denominations within those faiths approach the idea of relationships from various angles, each with its own beliefs and practices. This diversity in how relationships are viewed and practiced under the umbrella of religion is a testament to the multifaceted nature of human societies.

It challenges us to think beyond our preconceived notions and understand how people form bonds and families can be as diverse as their beliefs.

On that note, let's see how different societies view the whole non-monogamous relationship gig. We're not talking about a small corner of the world here; this is a global tour of *'who's doing what and how they're cool with it.'*

First stop, Western societies. You know, places like the good ol' U.S. of A., where monogamy is the billboard, but behind closed doors, it's a different show. Here, non-monogamy often gets the side-eye.

It's like, *"Do what you want, but don't flaunt it."*

Sure, there's a growing acceptance of different relationship dynamics, but it's still a bit hush-hush, you know?

Jump over to Europe, and it's a bit more laid back. In places like France, where love is as rich as their wine, they've got a more 'live and let live' attitude towards relationships. It's not a free-for-all, but they don't clutch their pearls at the idea of a ménage à trois scenario.

Now, let's swing by the Middle East and parts of Africa, where polygamy's part of the deal in many areas. It's not just accepted; it's often encouraged. But here's the catch – it's usually one guy with multiple wives. The ladies don't get to play the same game, which, honestly, doesn't sound like a fair deal.

Head over to Asia, and it's a mixed bag. You've got countries like China, where traditional values clash with modern love, creating a spectrum of relationship norms. Then there's India, where arranged marriages are still a thing, but so is swiping right on Tinder.

What's the point of this world tour of non-monogamy?

It's to show that this isn't just a *'Western'* or *'modern'* thing. It's a human thing. Different cultures have different ways of handling relationships, and that's okay. It's like a buffet – everyone's got their own taste, and no one's forced to eat the same dish.

So, before we jump into my wildlife story, remember this: non-monogamous relationships aren't just a trend or a rebellion against tradition. They're part of the human experience, varied and as complex as our societies. Whether it's openly accepted or whispered about, it's happening all around the globe. And that, folks, is a slice of real talk on how the world loves.

My name is Dr. Kam Asutra, and I am an expert on the subject of human sexual nature. It is said that once you have invested over 10k hours in a particular subject, you become an expert. I have had 15,683 hours of sex during my life. I am an expert.

People who venture into this type of relationship and often misunderstood territory are not just rebels without a cause but pioneers in redefining personal connections. But let's get something straight: it's not all roses and sunshine. There's a mix of benefits and challenges, though the scales tip more towards the former.

Firstly, freedom is the name of the game. We're talking about the kind of freedom that allows individuals to explore their desires without the confines of traditional expectations. It's like having your cake and eating it too, but with everyone at the table knowing and being cool. This openness can lead to a level of honesty that's sometimes missing in monogamous relationships.

You've got to lay your cards on the table; that kind of transparency can build stronger, more genuine connections.

Then there's the variety in experiences, emotions, and connections. It's like going to a buffet with endless dishes to try. Each relationship can fulfill different aspects of one's needs and desires. It's a journey of self-discovery, where you learn more about what makes you tick, both in and out of the bedroom.

The support network in non-monogamous relationships can be stronger, too. You're not just leaning on one person for emotional support; you've got a whole team. It's like having a personal cheer squad for your love life. This can create a web of care that's hard to replicate in a one-on-one scenario.

Now, it's not all a bed of roses.

The major challenge?

Jealousy. Managing jealousy requires emotional maturity and communication skills not everyone has in their toolkit. Your partner will be jealous whether you're open about it or do it secretly. It's like playing emotional Jenga – one wrong move, and things can come tumbling down.

At one time in my life, I was in three relationships at once. I had a wife, a girlfriend, and a mistress. My girlfriend knew about my wife but not about my mistress. On the other hand, my mistress knew about my wife and not my girlfriend. However, most importantly, my wife didn't know about it either. This way, I could keep all of them happy and satisfied, including myself.

This went great for seven years until my girlfriend married, and everything blew up. This was something I hadn't expected would happen.

Now, you have to understand that my girlfriend was my girlfriend before I met my wife and could have been my wife if things had been different. But, like life, things happen.

When I first met my girlfriend, she was married. I took her from her husband and made her my girlfriend. Right when I began to get serious about her, she cheated on me with her then ex-husband. After that, I met my wife and married her. More than likely, my girlfriend realized she would never be anything more than a girlfriend after I had married my wife. I mean, no one is. Even my wife was no angel - I will get to that later.

Now, back to my story.

Shortly after my first year of marriage, I acquired a mistress. This was not a reflection of my wife or our marriage. It was a simple case of me meeting a woman that I wanted to make mine. And so, I did just that: I made her mine.

At this point, you're probably wondering how the hell I managed to juggle and have time for three women at once, let alone finance three women.

To answer the first part of that question is very simple. Women are creatures of habit. A woman will patronize the same retail stores, restaurants, bars, etc., over and over. Her daily and weekly schedules are no different from the last; there's rarely any deviation from her habitual routine pattern.

With that in mind, it is easy to have a sense of creating red zones and blue zones. Red zones should be avoided, while blue zones are up for the taking. I know where my women are at all times, and when I am with one woman, I make sure that I do not go anywhere the other two women may frequent – I avoid the red zones.

To answer the second part of the question, I would have to answer the third one first: finances.

I have several lucrative businesses that have afforded me a lifestyle: if I wanted ten women, I could have ten women. As a result, I call the shots and play at will. I don't want to mislead you and think juggling multiple women is easy, either.

Having one woman is hard work in itself!

When you have multiple women, you must put in more effort and patience and always be alert. When I had been with one woman, I had to make sure her scent wasn't on me before I went home to my wife. When making love to any of them, I would have to consciously focus on the name of who I was fucking in that moment.

Needless to say, "Baby" became the universal name for all three women. Plus, focusing on my ejaculation was more important than remembering their names. Apart from that, I had to get three birthday, Christmas, and Valentine's gifts every year.

Did I mention the mood swings?

As soon as one got off her rag, the next one would be on hers. Having multiple women is a lot of work that's not for the weak.

As I said, life was good, and all three women were happy. At least, that's what I thought. I mean, none of them complained, except the usual, and the information gap of mistress knowing my girlfriend and wife and the rest worked perfectly. It was all fine till, as I mentioned, my girlfriend decided to get married.

One day, my girlfriend called and said she wanted to see me. In my head, I'm immediately thinking about the last time we hooked up.

Talk about fireworks!

Of course, I said, "Hell yeah, let's meet up!"

Then she said she had something to tell me. I heard the statement, but I wasn't really listening because I was still in my head, thinking of all the ways I was going to hit that pussy of hers. Slippery, when wet, should be tattooed right above her pussy.

I instructed her to meet me for drinks at my nightclub when she came into town before we went to the neighboring county's hotel room. Because of my marital status, this was a necessary precaution – my town was a red zone.

On the drive there, I felt something was off, and in hindsight, it was indeed off. She wasn't as frisky as she normally would be. But because of premeal instinct, her surfboard was the only thing front and center in my brain. I had some neo-soul playing on the car stereo as we coasted both along the highway and the Hennessy we had drunk.

When we entered the room, she sat on a chair in the corner of the suite with a somber look. Still refusing to acknowledge her social cues, I began removing my tie. When I sat on the bed to remove my shoes, she began to tell me that she was getting married and that she needed to know that if they fought, I'd be there for her.

In my mind, I couldn't care less. I was trying to pour the meat at that moment, which is exactly what I did after telling her what she wanted to hear.

Later, we got something to eat and then returned to the club. When the club closed, we returned to the room, where I continued to pour more meat. If you've never had the meat poured to your backside, I don't know what to tell you.

See, I'm at the point in my life where my dick doesn't get hard; it gets heavy. There is a difference – a big one and the ladies would understand.

Ladies, tell me, has he ever put it in, and then it gets so heavy that it cracks about three ribs?

That's where I'm at.

Back to my story, the next day, she went home. Now, you might be thinking, wait, that went pretty well… I told my girlfriend what she wanted to hear, got laid, and had the night over with her. How did it end my three relationships?

It all started that following Tuesday when I received several disturbing phone calls.

"Hey man, you were with my fiancé this weekend! You owe me $150.00 for the room she paid for. If you don't give me the money back, I'm telling your wife everything."

Then he hung up. I was floored. I couldn't believe it.

While trying to make sense of it all, the phone rang again. On this call, he proceeded to go into detail about how I fucked his fiancé. I listened in astonishment as he gave me a play-by-play.

"Y'all started in the bathroom with her sucking your dick. You were watching her slob all on your dick through the motel mirror. Then you led her to the bed, where you laid her down and climbed on top of her, pinning her legs up as high as they could go while thrusting yourself over and over into her with all your weight. Then you turned her over to doggy style, which must be your favorite position based on what she said."

As he continued to describe my night with his fiancé in vivid detail, I freaked out.

What else was he capable of doing?

I didn't know what to do or make of the situation. This wasn't normal at all!

I mean, who the hell listens to the details of their wife getting dicked down by another man, then blackmails the man by telling him how he got it on with his wife?

I was speechless.

Was my girlfriend a part of this and had set me up? What was going on?

Before I could make heads and tails of the situation, they got to my wife and told her everything. At that point, I couldn't lie because they'd sent her pictures we had taken that night. My wife had laid out my clothes that night. I couldn't get out of it.

Needless to say, my wife left me. I later found out she was seeing a guy she'd been going out with last year when we were together. So, I wasn't the only one who was cheating; she was, too, and so was my girlfriend.

Regardless, I had lost my wife and my girlfriend back-to-back.

So, I approached my mistress about promoting her to a more prestigious title – a wife or a girlfriend. Unfortunately, she was having none of it. Once she found out I didn't have a wife, she was no longer interested in our relationship. She explained that she never intended to be the number one in my life. She preferred being second in a man's life for her reasons. Not long after this conversation, she went on to find another married man.

What did I learn through my experiences?

I learned that everybody cheats regardless of the situation.

Is there an urge deep within us that causes us to find physical pleasure in others at some point in our monogamous relationships?

According to statistics, about 65 percent of people cheat.

So, I ask, what is wrong with those who are part of the 35 percent?

They may as well join those of us who are part of the 65 percent, so we can remove the word "cheat" from the dictionary entirely because one could argue that cheating is our basic instinct. Our basic animalistic instinct.

Let's wrap this chapter up with a bow and get the key takeaways front and center. This isn't just a bunch of words strung together; it's a reality check with a side of hard truths and eye-openers.

First, monogamy, the golden child of societal norms, isn't the only way to fly. Sure, it's been sold to us as the one-size-fits-all for relationships, but let's be real – it's not the universal fix it's cracked up to be. We've seen that in the animal kingdom, sticking to one partner is more of an exception than the rule.

So why are we, smarty-pants humans, trying to outsmart nature?

Then we rolled into the world of humans, where history tells us that polygamy wasn't just a thing; it was the thing. Kings, ordinary folk – you name it, they were doing it. Monogamy, the 'natural' way for humans, is a relatively new concept, more of a societal construct than a biological imperative.

And let's not sidestep the big, glaring issue of cheating. It's happening, and it's happening a lot. It's like we're all in a play where monogamy is the script, but a whole bunch of us are improvising.

That says something, doesn't it?

Maybe it's time to admit that monogamy isn't the end-all-be-all for everyone.

This chapter isn't just throwing shade at monogamy, though. It's about opening our eyes to the spectrum of relationships out there. It's about realizing that what works for one person might not work for another. Monogamy, polygamy, and everything in between – they're all part of the human experience.

We've also seen that non-monogamous relationships aren't just about having more sex (although that's a perk; let's not kid ourselves). In the grand scheme of things, this chapter is a wake-up call.

It's about questioning the status quo and understanding how we form bonds and families can be as diverse as our personalities. It's a call to be honest with ourselves and each other, to find what truly works for us in our relationships.

Just like Dr. (Zambuie) writes in his book *"There Is No Such Thing as Cheating,"* he explains that after a breakup, you should wait 90 days for every year you were in your last relationship for the healing process. He explains how it is necessary before one jumps into another relationship to avoid bringing baggage into the new relationship because they haven't fully healed. In this case, it is the only justifiable reason to apply the 90-day rule after a breakup.

Chapter 3: Marriage - the Cornerstone for Monogamy

Marriage stands at the forefront of our society, a tradition as old as civilization itself, often heralded as the ultimate commitment between two people. Yet, beneath its veneer of romantic idealism, marriage reveals itself as a complex institution, deeply intertwined with human sexuality, societal expectations, and personal fulfillment.

As we peel back the layers, we uncover that at its core, marriage is not just about love or companionship but also significantly about sex. It serves as a societal pillar, ostensibly designed to perpetuate the human species, wrapped in the allure of pleasure to ensure its continuation. This narrative starts from the beginning, with tales as old as Adam and Eve presented as the epitome of a monogamous union. However, whispers of discontent and the allure of forbidden fruits suggest that non-monogamy seeds were sown even in paradise.

The concept of marriage becomes a canvas upon which the human struggle with fidelity, desire, and societal norms is painted. It reflects the ongoing debate between the virtues of monogamy and the natural inclinations toward diversity in human relationships. This discourse isn't confined to the echoes of ancient stories or the hallowed halls of religious institutions; it resonates deeply with the lived experiences of individuals navigating the complexities of love and desire in the modern world.

The introduction of marriage into this conversation does not simplify the narrative to a binary choice between monogamy and non-monogamy but highlights the rich tapestry of human relationships. It challenges us to question the traditional pathways before us and consider the possibility that the human heart can love in more ways than one. This exploration is not just an academic exercise but a personal journey that delves into the essence of what it means to connect, love, and find fulfillment in the company of others.

As we venture into this discourse, it's essential to recognize that the institution of marriage, with all its complexities, serves as both a mirror and a mold. It reflects our deepest desires, fears, and biases while shaping how we perceive and engage in relationships. The conversation around marriage, monogamy, and non-monogamy is not just about societal norms but about the very nature of human connection and our endless pursuit of happiness.

In the modern era, this pursuit has led to a reevaluation of traditional relationship models, spurred by a deeper understanding of human psychology, changing social norms, and the advent of technology that has transformed how we meet, interact, and fall in love. This evolution prompts us to consider that perhaps the ancient framework of marriage needs to be revisited, not discarded, but expanded to encompass the diverse spectrum of human relationships and desires.

Thus, as we step into the following discourse, it is with the recognition that marriage, in its traditional and contemporary forms, offers a unique vantage point from which to examine the enduring questions of love, fidelity, and the human condition. It invites us to explore the myriad ways we seek connection, navigate the intimacy challenges, and ultimately strive to fulfill our deepest yearnings for companionship and understanding.

Marriage is pretty much about sex when you boil it down. It's got this big role in ensuring we keep the human race going, and apparently, it's been made fun to make sure we actually bother to do it. All this talk about Adam and Eve being the OG couple, setting up the whole one-on-one relationship deal. But then, there's a bunch of folks who think there was more drama in that garden than we're told. Maybe the serpent was another person, throwing a wrench into the whole Adam and Eve setup.

Some say it was Adam who got tempted by another woman, not just any woman, but one who was in cahoots with the devil. Imagine that, a twist where Adam's the one messing up and then trying to blame Eve. Classic move, right? And because of that, the devil throws a curse our way, ensuring we're always looking for the next thrill, never quite satisfied with just one partner. It's like saying, "You think you're perfect? Watch this."

So, this whole curse thing? It explains why sticking to one person is so challenging for many people. Thanks to some ancient screw-up, we're wired to crave variety. It's a bit of a kick in the teeth to the perfection concept, showing us that maybe we're not meant to be tied down to just one person.

This spin on the story makes you think twice about the whole monogamy thing, suggesting maybe we're not doing it wrong after all; perhaps we're just playing out the hand we were dealt. It's a way of looking at relationships that don't just accept the standard story but dig into the messy, complicated reality of what it means to be human and all the desires that come with it.

Taking this further, let's dive into why this whole monogamy versus non-monogamy debate is more than just about ancient curses or religious stories. It's about understanding human behavior and our needs on a deeper level. Think about it: humans are complex creatures with a wide range of desires and the need for connection. This isn't just about sex; it's about emotional fulfillment, adventure, and the quest for understanding ourselves and others.

Now, let's get real about the challenges monogamy brings. It's not just about staying faithful; it's about whether one person can meet all your needs - emotional, intellectual, and yes, sexual - for decades. That's a tall order. And with longer lifespans, the "till death do us part" promise stretches out even longer. People change, their desires evolve, and the idea that one partner can be everything might be outdated.

But here's where it gets interesting. The conversation about non-monogamy isn't about ditching commitment but redefining it. It's about honest communication, setting boundaries, and maybe finding that intimacy isn't limited to just one person. It's a different kind of trust and understanding that acknowledges our complex nature.

The rise of open relationships, polyamory, and other forms of non-monogamy shows that people are exploring new ways to structure their relationships. It's not for everyone, sure. But it's becoming clear that the traditional one-size-fits-all approach to relationships might not fit as well as we thought.

And let's not forget the role of technology in all of this. Dating apps, social media, and the internet have made meeting new people, exploring new relationships, and challenging the status quo easier. It's like the world has become this massive playground for exploring what we want and how we connect with others.

But here's the kicker: all of this exploration and questioning doesn't mean the end of love or commitment. If anything, it's about finding more authentic ways to experience them. It's about asking what works for you, not just following a script handed down through generations. Whether sticking with monogamy or charting a different course, it's all about finding what makes you and your partners happy and fulfilled.

It's not about condemning monogamy or glorifying non-monogamy. It's about understanding that relationships, like people, come in all shapes and sizes. And maybe, just maybe, the ancient stories and modern debates all point to the same thing: the need to understand and embrace our complexities, desires, and the many forms of love and connection that make life so rich and exciting.

I once did some research and discovered that in many societies, it was culturally practiced for men to sell their daughters into marriage. This can be found in the bible as well.

Women have always been seen as objects of desire or proprietary bargaining chips.

If a man had an ugly or obese daughter, he would pay another man to wed her. He would offer the man money, land, livestock, etc. The uglier or heavier she was, the higher the price would be.

She usually would do servitude work such as land cultivating, livestock care, or domestic work within the home.

Now, the arrangement is just the opposite if a woman is beautiful. A suitor offers her father money, land, livestock, etc. The prettier she is, the more money he has to offer for her.

Things really haven't changed too much, except women now use this as a blueprint to position themselves in a man's life. Men are driven by a woman's beauty and anatomy, which gives him sexual gratification, causing him to pay top dollar for her if she requires it. If she is fat or ugly, she will be doing good to get a McDonald's cheeseburger before she is sent on her way after being used as his cum hole.

This is what marriage is about. You may disagree, but I'm just telling it like it was and still is.

Let's unpack this, shall we? Regarding marriage and its aftermath, there are peculiar observations about the items we choose to frame or not. The marriage license, which is the official paper that seals the deal, often gets a prime spot on the wall. Yet, when the divorce papers roll in, marking the end of what was supposed to be forever, they rarely get the same treatment. Why is that? Is it because the symbol of union holds more weight than the freedom the divorce grants, or is it just that we value the beginning of stories more than their end?

Now, onto a spicier scenario. Imagine sitting down with your spouse for the most awkward conversation starter ever: questioning if there's a desire to get intimate with a friend. If he's got a pulse and an honest bone in his body, chances are he might just admit to fantasizing about your friend Sheni. Why Sheni, you ask? Well, it's not rocket science. You've seen the way he acts around her. All smiles, eager to lend a hand, sparking that gut feeling that something's up.

Flipping the script, what about when you prod your wife about her interest in your buddies? She'll likely shut that down fast, knowing they're just variations on your theme. But, bring the neighbor into the equation, the one she seems to dress up for under the guise of taking out the trash and watching the dynamics shift. It's all in the details, the subtle changes in behavior that scream volumes if you're paying attention.

These scenarios boil down to the unspoken truths and hidden desires lurking within relationships. It's about the honesty, or lack thereof, that can either make or break the trust between partners. The willingness to confront these uncomfortable truths head-on can be a real game-changer in understanding and navigating the complex dance of relationships. It's a messy, unpredictable journey, but it's also what makes the whole human connection thing so damn interesting.

Alright, circling back to the whole marriage gig, let's cut through the fluff. You both signed up for this ride, pledging to love, honor, and, yes, obey. But here's the kicker: if you're genuinely invested in your partner's happiness, the idea of an open relationship shouldn't send you running for the hills. Take Will and Jada, for example. They're like the poster couple for how an open setup can work for long-term happiness. And don't think it's just because they're rolling in dough and fame. This isn't about having the cash to smooth over problems; it's about honesty, trust, and maybe a dash of adventurous spirit.

The whole point is that an open relationship isn't for everyone, but should we dismiss it outright without considering its potential benefits? That's like refusing to try sushi because it's raw fish. You might just miss out on something that could spice up your life. It's all about setting boundaries, communicating like your relationship depends on it (because it does), and keeping an open mind.

The world's changing, folks. Relationships are evolving, and what works for one couple might be a no-go for another. But if one thing stays constant, it's the need for connection, understanding, and, let's be real, a bit of excitement. So, whether you're all in for monogamy, testing the waters of an open relationship, or somewhere in between, the bottom line is making sure it's making you and your partner genuinely happy and remembering how many of our receptors tell us that happiness is through having sex. Because, at the end of the day, that's what it's all about.

Earlier, we touched on how various religions and cultures embrace polygamy, but let's not leave Group Marriage out in the cold. Imagine a setup where the concept of "my better half" gets an ensemble cast—multiple wives multiple husbands, all under one roof. Think of it as swinging but with a twist of long-term commitment.

Now, for a bit of a reality check, courtesy of the American Association for Marriage and Family Therapy, marital infidelity tops the charts as the leading cause of divorce. The numbers are eye-opening, with a significant slice of men and a notable percentage of women in the study confessing to extramarital alliances. And let's be honest, the real stats are probably playing hide and seek with the truth.

Here's where I throw in my two cents, old-school style: Deny, deny, deny. But beneath that mantra lies a bigger question—why do so many find themselves straying? Could it be that the traditional mold of monogamy, as revered as it is, doesn't quite fit the human condition as snugly as we've been led to believe?

Consider this: if the natural world and history itself are anything to go by, humans' flirtation with monogamy might be more of a modern experiment than a timeless truth. The animal kingdom, with its freewheeling approach to partnerships, and the annals of human societies, rich with tales of polygamy, suggest that exclusivity isn't the only game in town.

So, where does that leave us?

It would be interesting to know what the divorce statistics would be if Polygamy were our way of life.

Diving into the gritty details of Vicki Leon's research, we're slapped with the harsh realities of ancient Athens and Rome, where cheaters faced death or, bizarrely, radish retribution. It's a stark reminder of how seriously these societies took the sanctity of marriage vows—so much so that infidelity could literally cost you your dignity or, more graphically, a comfortable sitting posture.

Fast forward to contemporary America, where divorce rates paint a telling picture of monogamy's shortcomings. The idea that humans are naturally inclined to stick with just one partner for life seems increasingly fanciful against the backdrop of rising infidelity statistics. It begs the question: are we fighting against our inherent nature by enforcing monogamy as the gold standard?

Leon's reflection on ancient punishments for adultery might seem outlandishly irrelevant at first glance. Yet, it underscores a critical point—humans have always struggled with fidelity. If the threat of death or a radish didn't stop cheaters back then, are the modern-day stigma and legal complications of divorce really going to keep partners faithful?

This brings us to a broader conversation about human sexuality and relationship dynamics. The evidence suggests a disconnect between societal expectations of monogamy and the natural inclinations of many individuals toward multiple partners. The ancient Greeks and Romans, with their severe penalties for infidelity, recognized this tension but addressed it in ways that are unimaginable today.

In proposing a shift towards a more polygamous understanding of relationships, we confront the reality that monogamy might not be the one-size-fits-all solution it's touted to be. If the goal is genuine happiness and fulfillment in relationships, perhaps it's time to acknowledge that this could mean the freedom to explore connections with multiple partners for many.

The discussion isn't about endorsing infidelity but rather recognizing that the traditional framework of monogamy might be too rigid for the diverse range of human desires and needs. By opening up the dialogue to include polygamy and other forms of non-monogamous relationships, we can begin to construct a more inclusive, realistic understanding of love and partnership.

Reflecting on the extreme measures of ancient societies to curb adultery, juxtaposed with the modern reality of divorce and dissatisfaction in monogamous relationships, it's evident that a reevaluation of our relationship norms is overdue. The exploration of polygamy not as a relic of the past but as a viable contemporary choice could be the key to aligning our societal structures with the complex nature of human desires and relationships.

Why are we even talking about this? It's not like we're sitting in a history class. The point isn't to give a history lesson but to highlight a crucial aspect of human nature: the inclination towards multiple partners is not a modern development influenced by the internet or contemporary society. This behavior traces back to the earliest humans, suggesting that cheating and seeking multiple partners is as old as humanity itself. The internet has merely amplified our awareness of infidelity by providing a platform for sharing personal experiences and grievances. However, this focus on digital revelations obscures a fundamental truth about human behavior.

Contrary to popular belief, humans are not inherently monogamous. Our biological makeup drives us toward maximizing reproductive opportunities. This isn't about moral judgment but an observation rooted in evolutionary biology. In a biological context, ' fitness' refers to an individual's genetic success, measured by the number of offspring they produce. Thus, from a biological standpoint, the more partners one has, the greater one's opportunity for reproductive success; hence, the more fit one becomes.

The concept of fitness associated with physical prowess or athleticism is a modern interpretation. Biologically, being 'fit' means having a higher number of descendants. This perspective shifts the idea of success from physical achievements to reproductive success.

In historical context, Genghis Khan is often cited as an example of this biological fitness. His legacy isn't just in conquests but in his genetic footprint, having fathered many children across the territories he conquered. This example illustrates that reproductive success and the drive to propagate one's genes have historically been significant factors in human behavior.

Where I'm going with this is that no matter the reasons for the infidelity, sex was the go-to. Any excuse will do. We are driven by sex, and I can't reiterate enough that if the sex is no good, the relationship will be affected. Therefore, the 90-day rule is a setup for failure and a tool for a manipulator. If a woman knows her sex game is wack, it will be this very woman that will push the 90-day agenda or that wait to we're married bullshit. Because she's hoping that by the time you find out her sex is trash, it won't matter to you. Why? Because you are emotionally locked in now. The Gold Digger also pushes this agenda, but that's another conversation that makes me think of the individual who does too much at the beginning of a new relationship.

See, they throw everything but the kitchen sink at you, hoping something sticks. It's a smokescreen, a distraction from what's happening—or not—in the bedroom. This tactic, my friends, is as old as time, yet it's got a new polish in today's world where everyone's trying to sell you an image. But let's not kid ourselves: when the chips are down, and the novelty wears off, you're left with the raw truth. And if that truth doesn't include mind-blowing sex, well, you're in for a rude awakening.

It's this simple: sex is the glue that holds a relationship together. And if someone's pushing you to wait without a taste of what's to come, you've got to wonder what they're hiding. It's not about being shallow; it's about being real with what you want and what you're getting into. No one wants to find out they've signed up for a lifetime subscription to mediocre sex after the fact. That's why these games people play, like the 90-day rule or the marriage-first agenda, are nothing but traps, cleverly disguised to rope you in before you realize what you've signed up for.

And let's not forget about those who overcompensate at the start. They lay it on thick, showering you with gifts, attention, and promises of a fairy-tale romance. But it's all a performance, a carefully choreographed dance to distract you from their shortcomings. It's a tactic as transparent as it is desperate and designed to hook you emotionally before you see behind the curtain.

We're talking about a fundamental disconnect between expectations and reality, fueled by societal norms that no longer serve us. The sooner we acknowledge that sexual compatibility is a cornerstone of a healthy relationship, not an optional extra, the better off we'll be. Let's cut through the BS and get real about what makes or breaks a connection. It's high time we ditched the outdated rules and started talking about what matters.

Have you ever had a woman love you so much that it starts feeling like too much? Yes, it's possible to drown in love that tries too hard. Picture this: everything she does, no matter how sweet or well-meaning, turns into a disaster. Things could run smoothly if she just took a breath and relaxed a little. But nope, it's like being stuck in a cycle of mishaps, a lousy movie on constant replay. Why would anyone keep subjecting themselves to that kind of chaos? It makes zero sense.

Imagine coming home from work, the day's stress melting away as you think about the game you'll watch and the cold beers waiting in the fridge. But as you step in, ready for that moment of relaxation, she hits you with, "I've prepared a bath for you," only to discover the bathroom's flooded because she forgot the water running. So much for unwinding, right? Now, your evening's about cleaning up, not chilling out. And just as you think it can't get worse, you smell something burning. The dinner, which was supposed to be a simple, enjoyable part of the evening, is now a charred mess, setting off the fire alarm and sprinklers, adding a flood to your already-soaked apartment.

Situations like these, where the effort to do something nice ends up in chaos, make you question the whole setup. This isn't just about a flooded bathroom or a burnt dinner; the relentless attempt to do too much is the issue. It's like there's no off switch, and every attempt at doing something special becomes a potential disaster.

The thing is, love shouldn't feel like you're constantly trying to avert crises. When someone loves you too much to the point where their efforts become counterproductive, it's a signal to reassess. Sure, intentions might be pure, but when every gesture becomes a potential catastrophe, it's clear something's gotta give. It's about finding balance, not living on the edge of the next disaster.

While possibly coming from a good place, this overzealous love often feels suffocating rather than supportive. It's a lesson in moderation, in understanding that sometimes less is more and that trying too hard can push things in the opposite direction of where they were meant to go.

Chapter 4: Polygamy vs. Monogamy

Monogamy's roots dig deep, going back over a thousand years, standing as the legally recognized norm in the U.S.—a bond exclusively between one man and one woman until not too long ago. Some Christians see it as a lifelong commitment, unbreakable until death does its part. But that's old news. The real kicker? Polygamy. Let's dive into the juicy details without mincing words.

Polygamy isn't just a footnote in history; it's a whole chapter that's been glossed over. While monogamy got the spotlight, polygamy was the norm in many cultures around the globe. It wasn't just about having multiple partners for the heck of it; it was about economics, politics, and social structure. In many societies, it was about building alliances, managing wealth, or ensuring descendants. In others, it was simply a matter of social status.

But here's the kicker: polygamy, in its various forms, has been around way longer than monogamy's claim to fame. From the kings and pharaohs of ancient civilizations to tribal leaders and common folk, multiple spouses were part of the deal. And it wasn't all male-centric either. Some cultures practiced polyandry, where a woman might have multiple husbands. Talk about flipping the script!

Now, fast forward to today. Polygamy's seen as taboo, a relic of the past that modern society can't quite stomach. But why? We've all agreed to pretend this part of human history and culture doesn't fit the neat narrative we've constructed around relationships and love.

But let's cut to the chase: polygamy challenges the conventional. It dares to question the one-size-fits-all approach to relationships that society has been selling us. Sure, it's not for everyone. But neither is monogamy.

It's about breaking the mold, challenging the status quo, and acknowledging that love has always been complex in its many forms. Polygamy isn't just a spicy topic for debates; it's a testament to the vast spectrum of human connections. And while it might not be everyone's cup of tea, it's part of the conversation on relationships that deserves its due—unfiltered, bold, and with a dash of humor because the history of human relationships is anything but monochrome.

Polygamy and The Bible

Polygamy isn't just a relic of ancient times; it's as American as apple pie—or at least as American as Joseph Smith and the early days of Mormonism. Now, if you think polygamy in the U.S. is a recent phenomenon, think again. The practice dates back to 1830, kicking off with Joseph Smith, who not only founded the Mormon movement but also introduced polygamy as a spicy addition to the religious menu on July 12, 1843. And boy, did it stir the pot.

Smith's take on polygamy wasn't just about adding flavor to religious practices but also redefining the entire recipe. To him, having multiple wives wasn't just acceptable; it was a divine mandate. But let's be real: this sounded like a convenient excuse for a free-for-all in the bedroom to outsiders. Smith and his cohorts enjoyed their secret sauce for over two decades until Brigham Young, then church president, decided to share their culinary secrets with the world. In 1852, he had Orson Pratt, one of the Twelve Apostles, go public and defend plural marriage. Imagine the gossip at the water cooler that day.

Smith's lifestyle, hidden for twenty-two years, suddenly under the microscope, must have shocked the system. Here was a man caught between his "biblical practices" and the hard reality of living a life that was, to say the least, unconventional. Christians, after all, are big on the one-man-one-woman model, citing verses like *1 Timothy 3:12* and *Titus 1:6.* But, as always, interpretation is critical. As they say, the devil is in the details—or, in this case, the fine print of religious texts.

Smith's mental gymnastics to justify his lifestyle choices would have made an Olympic athlete proud. He had to convince his followers and perhaps himself that what they were doing was A-OK in the eyes of the Lord. It's the kind of reasoning that makes you wonder whether divine inspiration or human desire is the real driving force.

Joseph Smith's legacy is as complicated as the man himself. On one hand, he was a visionary leader who charted a new religious path. On the other, he was a man whose personal life choice sparked controversy, debate, and, let's face it, a fair amount of side-eye.

Whether you see him as a prophet or a provocateur, one thing's for sure: when it comes to polygamy in America, Joseph

Smith and his merry band of polygamists were pioneers, for better or worse.

Polygamy in the Bible and its interpretation, particularly through verses like *1 Timothy 3:12* and *Titus 1:6,* opens up a fascinating dialogue about biblical teachings' historical and cultural contexts and their application to contemporary beliefs and practices.

1 Timothy 3:12 states, *"Let deacons each be the husband of one wife, managing their children and their own households well."*

Similarly, **Titus 1:6** includes criteria for church leaders, stating, *"If anyone is above reproach, the husband of one wife, and his children are believers and not open to the charge of debauchery or insubordination."*

Both these verses are part of the pastoral epistles, providing guidance for church leadership and household management within the early Christian communities.

The directive for a church leader to be the "husband of one wife" has been interpreted in several ways. The most straightforward interpretation suggests a call for marital fidelity and stable family life for those in leadership positions. It emphasizes monogamy as a virtue, especially in a cultural context where polygamy is not uncommon. This requirement was likely intended to set a moral and ethical example for the community, underscoring the importance of a singular, committed marital relationship as a foundation for social and religious leadership.

However, some scholars argue that these passages do not outright condemn polygamy; instead, they focus on the moral and ethical qualifications for leadership within the church. The emphasis on being the husband of one wife can also be seen as a call for order and stability in a leader's personal life, reflecting on their ability to lead within the church.

Furthermore, the historical context of these texts is crucial. At the time these letters were written, polygamy was a practice in many cultures, including Jewish society. The early Christian church was establishing its identity and norms, often in contrast to or in negotiation with surrounding cultural practices. By advocating for leaders to have one wife, the apostle Paul (traditionally attributed as the author of these epistles) could have advocated for a new Christian ethos that emphasized specific family structures as more conducive to the health and order of the Christian community.

In the broader biblical context, polygamy is present, with several key figures, such as Abraham, Jacob, David, and Solomon, having multiple wives. These instances are descriptive of the practices of the time rather than prescriptive for all followers. The New Testament, however, does not record any endorsements of polygamy and, through passages like those in 1 Timothy and Titus, seems to lean towards monogamy, especially for those in leadership positions within the church.

Modern Polygamy

Polygamy walks the streets in sneakers and a hoodie, easily blending and mixing into the crowd. It's not the overt, multiple-marriage scenario of yesteryears but a more covert operation.

Hidden in plain sight, it thrives in the gray areas of relationships, often with participants unaware of their shared connections. The echoes of polygamy resonate through rap music, social media, and films, promoting a culture of multiple sexual partners under the guise of modernity and freedom.

This societal trend isn't just about having a backup plan for Friday night. It's a reflection of a deeper, more ingrained perspective on relationships. My dad once dropped this truth bomb: expecting a man to stick with one woman is like asking him to swim upstream, against his very nature. Shahrazad Ali doubles down on this, insisting that a man's heart is too wild for just one partner.

While our society officially wears the monogamy badge, the reality on the ground tells a different story. The only voices championing monogamy seem to come from religious corners, which, ironically, are the foundation of the laws that still brand polygamy as illegal. But let's not kid ourselves: the mainstream media isn't exactly putting up a fight to keep the monogamy ship sailing.

So, where does that leave us? In a strange limbo, where, on the one hand, having multiple partners is as normalized as binge-watching Netflix series, and on the other, the law is wagging its finger at the very notion of multiple marriages. It's as if society is playing a game of "do as I say, not as I do," promoting serial monogamy with a polygamous twist.

This duality presents a peculiar modern dilemma: we're encased in a monogamist legal framework while culturally winking at polygamy. The disparity between what's preached and what's practiced is stark, revealing a societal split personality.

The bottom line?

While the law books may not have caught up, the human script is being rewritten every day. This isn't about advocating for one lifestyle over another but acknowledging human relationships' complex, layered nature. Whether we admit it or not, the essence of polygamy—minus the marriage certificates— is woven into the fabric of contemporary society, challenging us to rethink our definitions of commitment, love, and fidelity in the 21st century.

Diving deeper into the heart of modern relationships reveals a landscape far more complex than the simple dichotomy of legal monogamy versus cultural polygamy. This isn't just about the legal bindings of marriage or the casual flings celebrated in pop culture; it's about the evolving nature of human connections in a world where traditional labels no longer apply.

Consider the role of technology in this transformation. Dating apps and social media have revolutionized how we meet, interact, and maintain relationships, enabling accessibility and variety that previous generations could hardly imagine. Connections are made and broken with a swipe or a click, fostering an environment where exclusivity can often be more of an ideal than a reality. This digital landscape has blurred the lines between monogamy and polygamy, creating a new normal where the number of partners one may have been limited only by the battery life of their smartphone.

In this context, the traditional concept of polygamy seems almost quaint. Why bother with the formality of multiple marriages when the digital age offers a buffet of relational styles, from open relationships to polyamory, without the need for any legal acknowledgment?

This shift isn't just a change in practice but a fundamental rethinking of what it means to be in a relationship. It's a move away from possession and exclusivity towards a model based on mutual respect, freedom, and, for some, an acknowledgment of the impracticality of expecting one person to meet all another's needs and desires.

Yet, this shift comes with its own set of challenges. The freedom to form connections with multiple partners can lead to unforeseen complexities and complications in more traditional relationship structures. Jealousy, time management, and negotiating boundaries take on new dimensions in this landscape. Moreover, the societal stigma attached to non-monogamous relationships can lead to misunderstandings and judgments from those outside these arrangements, often overshadowing the potential benefits with a cloud of controversy.

Furthermore, the conversation around modern polygamy and its casual counterpart in society forces a reevaluation of the values we hold dear in relationships. It calls into question the sustainability of traditional models in the face of human nature's diversity and the ever-evolving social fabric. This isn't an argument for the superiority of one style over another but a recognition of the need for a broader understanding and acceptance of the myriad ways people choose to connect and form bonds.

The current state of relationships reflects a broader cultural shift towards individual choice and away from one-size-fits-all solutions. As society continues to evolve, so too will our understanding and acceptance of the various forms love and connection can take. It's a journey that challenges us to think critically about what we value in our relationships and how those values align with the realities of the modern world. The future of human connection may be uncertain, but it's undeniably rich with possibilities.

Benefits of Having a Polygamous Relationship

In the kaleidoscope of modern relationships, polygamy isn't just about the romance or the drama—it's also about the dollars and cents. That's right, some folks are looking at polygamy through a pragmatic lens, seeing it as more than just a complex web of relationships. For them, it's akin to a startup business where everyone on the team has a stake in its success. Enter the concept of the "New Kingston Clan," a metaphorical nod to those who approach polygamy not just as a lifestyle choice but as a financial strategy.

This isn't about throwing traditional values to the wind; it's about recognizing the potential for mutual benefit in a setup where all participants are on board and invested in the outcome. Think of it as a communal living arrangement where resources are pooled, responsibilities are shared, and financial burdens are lightened. It's about leveraging the collective power of the group to achieve economic stability and prosperity—a far cry from the stereotype of polygamy as merely a hedonistic free-for-all.

In these arrangements, each member brings something to the table—income, skill sets, or resources—making the collective stronger and more resilient than the sum of its parts. It's a savvy acknowledgment of the economic challenges many face today, where single-income households are increasingly a thing of the past, and the cost of living continues to soar.

The "New Kingston Clan" is emblematic of a broader trend: the reimagining of traditional relationship structures in response to modern economic realities. It's a bold assertion that love, commitment, and financial pragmatism can coexist, challenging the monogamous paradigm not only on a romantic or sexual level but also on a fiscal one.

Critics might balk at the idea, dismissing it as cold or calculating, but proponents see it as a practical solution to the financial strains of contemporary life. This approach to polygamy underscores a broader shift towards questioning and redefining the norms that govern our personal and financial lives.

It's not just about who you love; it's also about how you navigate the world together. The "new Kingston Clan" represents a movement towards a more deliberate and strategic approach to relationships, where the heart and the wallet are not at odds but in alignment, offering a fresh perspective on how to build a life that's both emotionally fulfilling and economically sound.

The Consequences

The landscape of relationships is shifting, and polygamy is spreading its wings, embracing a wider array of forms than the traditional one-man-many-women setup. It's creeping into the LGBTQ+ community, redefining what a polygamist relationship looks like in today's world. What's on the rise is an "Open Relationship," a term becoming as common as complaining about traffic.

But here's the rub: kids are entering the picture. And not just a few here and there, but entire squads. You might shrug and say, "So what?" Well, the "what" is the glaring absence of fathers from these children's lives. I'm talking about the Nick Cannons, the Jocs of the world, and your garden-variety town player.

Sure, Nick Cannon and Joc might have the means to ensure their nine kids each don't want anything material. But what about the mental and emotional stuff? Can a dad with a Rolodex of businesses really dish out the quality time needed for emotional and mental development?

With their packed schedules, it's a wonder they find time to even contribute to the baby-making process.

And then there's our friend, the town philanderer, playing the same game but without the financial cushion. This guy's a piece of work, often tangled in his web of narcissism, treating the creation of life as just another notch on his belt—a regrettable byproduct of his conquests. The damage goes beyond neglected kids, spiraling into deceit, broken hearts, and the spread of STDs.

This lifestyle isn't just a modern-day dilemma; it's a historical headache with long-term repercussions, especially for the kids caught in the crossfire. The polygamist community, founded on the notion that prolific procreation is next to godliness, doesn't account for the emotional bankruptcy it leaves in its wake. The idea that a man could father scores of children across multiple wives isn't just logistically ludicrous; it's emotionally catastrophic.

Imagine being one of sixty kids vying for a slice of Dad's attention. It's not a stretch to say these children often end up feeling like they're more part of a crowd than a family. No matter how broad your shoulders are, there's only so much love and time you can give. The arithmetic of affection doesn't add up when you spread it thinly across an army of offspring.

So, while polygamy and open relationships march into the future, waving the flag of freedom and financial savvy, we've got to ask ourselves about the cost, not just in dollars, but in the currency of connection, presence, and emotional support. As these unconventional relationships evolve, so must our understanding of responsibility, especially when the legacy we leave behind is measured in human hearts, not just bank accounts.

Chapter 5: Bread Dildo

Pythagoras, the ancient Greek sage, catapulted into fame not solely through his philosophical musings but more so with a theorem that dramatically transformed the world of geometry. This theorem, stating that the area of the square built upon the hypotenuse of a right-angled triangle is equal to the combined areas of the squares erected on the other two sides, unveiled a groundbreaking insight.

This revelation, though it appears straightforward, casts a profound illumination on geometric principles, asserting that the dimensions of a triangle are decipherable with the knowledge of a right angle. Intriguingly, this ancient mathematical insight seems to resonate with the modern, albeit unconventional, Dildo Bread Theorem, weaving together not just the elements of matter and time but also hinting at a deeper, somewhat risqué connection known as the *oooweee* effect.

The leap from Pythagoras' geometric foundations to the Dildo Bread Theorem might strike one as a jump across realms — from the austere corridors of mathematics to the provocative alleys of sexual innuendo. Yet, this transition is less about abandoning rigor for ribaldry and more about embracing the diverse ways human intellect and inventiveness manifest. The Dildo Bread Theorem, much like its geometric counterpart, underscores a universal truth: that underlying patterns and principles can be discerned within the most unexpected of contexts.

This theorem, cloaked in humor and audacity, serves as a playful juxtaposition and a metaphorical bridge linking the empirical with the experiential. It suggests that the laws governing the physical world are not confined to the abstract or the celestial but are intimately connected to the corporeal and the carnal. In this light, the theorem emerges as a cheeky nod to the idea that human creativity and curiosity know no bounds, extending their reach from the platonic to the pragmatic, from the realm of ideal forms to that of earthly delights.

The dialogue engendered by juxtaposing Pythagoras' theorem with the concept of Dildo Bread ventures beyond mere entertainment or shock value. It embodies a deliberate provocation, a challenge to the reader to reconsider the boundaries between the sacred and the profane, the serious and the frivolous. This discourse, replete with directness, colloquial charm, and bold assertions, not only captivates but also compels a deeper engagement with the material, encouraging a critical, albeit amused, reflection on the complexities of human knowledge and desire.

Moreover, the empowerment inherent in this thematic exploration — asserting personal agency and sexual autonomy against mathematical and philosophical inquiry — underscores a radical departure from traditional narratives. By infusing the discussion with explicit content and challenging social norms, the narrative fosters a space where taboo subjects are not only broached but examined with candor and wit.

Expanding the content to include the Dildo Bread Theorem within the Pythagorean discourse is an exercise in intellectual dexterity. It leverages humor, analogy, and provocative thought to bridge disparate worlds, inviting readers to appreciate the richness and complexity of human thought and its application across the spectrum of existence — from the geometric to the erotic, from the realm of numbers to the domain of pleasure.

Delving into the Babylonian Talmud, we uncover a passage that presents an extraordinary use of bread, not for nourishment, but as a medicinal implement crafted to provoke ejaculation. This intriguing advice, offered by Rav Yosef bar Hiyya, suggests that for individuals afflicted by an obstruction of the external urethral orifice, the placement of warm dildo bread upon the anus could incite semen flow, thereby alleviating the blockage. This novel application of heat and ancient medical insight illuminates the sophisticated ways our forebears merged culinary expertise with therapeutic knowledge.

This intersection of food and medicine, as peculiar as it appears, serves as a testament to the innovative spirit of ancient civilizations in addressing health concerns. It showcases a time when the boundaries between different spheres of knowledge were fluid, allowing creative solutions to emerge from the most unexpected places. The use of dildo bread, specifically, highlights a fascinating aspect of human ingenuity, where everyday items were repurposed in the service of medical treatments, reflecting a deep understanding of the body's responses to various stimuli.

Moreover, mentioning this unique practice in such a respected and ancient text as the Babylonian Talmud adds a layer of historical credibility to the narrative, suggesting that the ancients possessed a more complex and nuanced approach to sexuality and health than is often credited. The blending of culinary skills with medicinal practices underscores a holistic view of health care, where the benefits of warmth, the tactile nature of bread, and the psychological comfort provided by familiar objects were all leveraged to treat a delicate condition.

This exploration into the use of dildo bread as a medicinal tool not only broadens our understanding of ancient medical practices but also invites us to reconsider our modern approaches to health and healing. It encourages a reflection on the potential of combining traditional wisdom with contemporary medical knowledge to enhance our well-being.

By revisiting these ancient practices, we are reminded of the value of cross-disciplinary innovation and the importance of viewing health through a broad lens that includes physical, psychological, and cultural dimensions. The example of Rav Yosef bar Hiyya and his unconventional prescription offers a compelling narrative about the adaptability and resourcefulness of our ancestors, inspiring for today's health practitioners to think outside the conventional medical box.

Enter Vicki L. Ho, a modern-day historian with a flair for uncovering the obscure. Ho narrates the tale of how the dildo breadstick, potentially the world's inaugural sex toy, came into being in an Athenian bakery. A young woman, perhaps overwhelmed by time and creativity, melded bread dough into the shape of an olisbo-kollix while lost in reverie. This invention, discreet and easily disposed of, became a cherished companion for the women of Athens, offering a solution to their unmet desires. Like a black widow spider, the creator of such a device would move on to craft another, leaving behind a legacy of innovation and satisfaction.

Building on this foundation, the narrative deepens as we consider the broader implications of such an invention in the context of ancient Athens, a city-state known for its philosophical inquiries and artistic expressions. The emergence of the dildo breadstick, as chronicled by Vicki L. Ho, speaks volumes about Athenian society's approach to sexuality and innovation. It suggests an environment where creativity was not confined to the realms of the arts and philosophy but extended into the intimate corners of daily life, embodying the essence of human curiosity and the pursuit of personal fulfillment.

Ho's recounting also prompts a reflection on the role of women in ancient societies, often overlooked or underestimated by historical narratives. The young woman behind the olisbo-kollix becomes a symbol of female agency, using the resources at her disposal to address a need unspoken yet universally felt among her peers. This act of creation, veiled in the anonymity of history, highlights the ingenuity and resilience of women navigating the constraints of their time.

Moreover, the story of the dildo breadstick, as brought to light by Vicki L. Ho, challenges our contemporary understanding of ancient civilizations, urging us to rethink our assumptions about their norms and values, especially regarding sexuality. It showcases how ancient peoples engaged with the same fundamental desires and needs that concern us today, albeit through different means and expressions.

In essence, the tale of the dildo breadstick, as narrated by Vicki L. Ho, enriches our understanding of human history, weaving together threads of creativity, sexuality, and female empowerment. It serves as a reminder that history is not just the study of past events but a continuous dialogue between the past and present, offering insights and reflections that resonate with our experiences and challenges. Through this lens, the story of an ancient breadstick transcends its initial curiosity, becoming a profound commentary on the human condition.

Chapter 6: Own Your Pussy

Ladies, y'all haven't owned your pussy since Louis IIIV cut off Queen Elizabeth's head. After which, women began ducking their heads with their asses in the air, coining the phrase *Ass Up, Head Down*. Because hell, who's trying to cut your head off if your ass is tooted up in the air?

In this realm where power dictates the game and those at the helm craft the rules, it's undeniable that sexuality harbors its formidable influence. This truth, as ancient as time itself, reveals that the allure and strength of sexuality can sway decisions, alter fates, and challenge the very fabric of societal constructs. The narrative isn't new, yet it remains as compelling as ever, underscoring the undeniable force that sexuality, particularly feminine sexuality, wields in the grand scheme of human interaction.

Consider the age-old adage, often whispered but universally acknowledged: the person holding power pens the rules. Yet, what's usually overlooked is the subtle yet profound power of feminine allure. This isn't just about allure in a physical sense, but the profound capability to influence, steer decisions and actions, and in many ways, to hold an unspoken sway over dynamics traditionally dominated by brute strength or authority. It's a testament to the nuanced yet potent forms of influence that go beyond the physical, tapping into the psychological and emotional realms.

Reflect on the candid confession of a man so captivated, so utterly enchanted by feminine allure, that he professed a willingness to meet his demise at its behest. This admission isn't merely about the physical act but speaks volumes about the profound impact of feminine charm and allure. It's a raw, unfiltered acknowledgment of the power dynamics at play, often subverted and underestimated in their influence.

James Brown's timeless tune, "Caldonia," is a poignant illustration of this phenomenon. The song narrates a tale of a man, warned by his mother to steer clear of Caldonia, yet so mesmerized by her essence that he chooses to defy maternal counsel. It's a narrative that echoes through ages, a vivid illustration of the magnetic pull of feminine allure, capable of making a grown man rebel against the foundational advice of his upbringing.

This narrative isn't merely about rebellion or its physical aspects; it's a deeper commentary on the power dynamics underpinning human relationships. The song, much like the tales that weave through the fabric of our society, highlights the intricate dance between autonomy, desire, and societal expectations.

The power vested in sexuality, particularly within the context of feminine allure, extends beyond mere physical interaction. It's about influence, autonomy, and the subtle yet undeniable sway it holds over societal norms and individual actions. This power can reshape destinies, redefine paths, and challenge the constructs of power traditionally recognized.

In broaching these subjects, the dialogue opens up a broader conversation about autonomy, influence, and the inherent power dynamics that shape our interactions and societal structures. It's a testament to the complex interplay of desires, societal norms, and the undervalued power of sexuality in navigating the intricate human experience. This discourse isn't just about challenging norms but about acknowledging and embracing the multifaceted dimensions of human interaction and the subtle powers that govern it.

The powers that be, who craft the rules of society, possess a keen awareness of sexuality's influential role in politics and power dynamics, thus anchoring their dominance. They ingeniously devise regulations that, while seemingly universal, are tailored to bolster their positions of authority, skillfully manipulating societal norms to their advantage. This manipulation extends across genders, though women, despite often being the more astute, find themselves more susceptible to such influences, not due to a lack of intelligence but because of their emotional capacity.

While a source of strength, this emotional depth also renders women more vulnerable to manipulation. By appealing to their passions and concerns of the moment, those in power can sway female perspectives and actions to align with broader agendas, such as those witnessed in movements like Me Too. While the Me-Too movement marked a significant stride towards acknowledging and addressing sexual misconduct, it also serves as a poignant example of how emotional appeals can be harnessed to shift societal focus. The movement, ostensibly a triumph for female empowerment, raises questions about the true extent of its impact on women's autonomy over their bodies and choices.

The narrative of women's leveraging their sexuality for economic gain, only to later seek legal redress, encapsulates a broader strategy employed by the elite to divide and rule, perpetuating cycles of manipulation. While offering temporary victories, this strategy often obscures the underlying power dynamics, leading to a superficial sense of empowerment that fails to address the root causes of inequality and exploitation.

In this context, the concept of true empowerment and autonomy is complex. It extends beyond the legal victories against perpetrators of sexual misconduct to encompass a deeper understanding and assertion of one's value and rights. A woman who comprehends the game's intricacies opts not for the courtroom but for strategic navigation within the system, ensuring her compensation reflects her worth from the outset. This approach negates the need for retrospective legal battles, embodying a form of empowerment that transcends the superficial gains touted by societal movements.

The depiction of men involved in these dynamics as either 'creepy' or driven by hypersexuality oversimplifies a multifaceted issue. It fails to account for the nuanced realities of sexual desire, consent, and power. The framing of these men as villains in a narrative of female victimhood overlooks the broader societal structures that commodify sexuality, reducing complex human interactions to transactions devoid of mutual respect and understanding.

Thus, the discourse surrounding sexuality, power, and manipulation is symbolic of the broader struggles against patriarchal systems. It highlights the need for a more nuanced understanding of consent, autonomy, and empowerment, challenging us to reconsider the narratives we endorse and the mechanisms of control we inadvertently perpetuate.

Women respect resources. It is their nature. Nature's law. Provide a woman with all her needs; you will have very little pushback from her, if any. Kanye West's song "Gold Digger" describes the average woman and therefore is mistitled. Every woman wants to be protected and provided for. Even if she has her own money, she wants the protection and provision of her man.

This will be a high-value man. He financially provides for her without her asking for anything, as well as providing mental stimulation. She has a life issue or crisis going on; he fixes it. She is looking for a savior, a daddy, and Jody wrapped in one. Give her this, and she will genuinely consider doing anything this man suggests that she do. Ten out of ten times, the woman will do whatever it is so that she does not lose this security, even if it's something she would never do, such as Polygamy.

Expanding on this, the societal construct that underpins these relationships is deeply rooted in traditional views on gender roles and economic stability. The notion that a woman's security, and by extension her willingness to explore unconventional relationship structures such as polygamy, hinges on the financial and emotional support provided by a man opens a broader dialogue about the dynamics of power and autonomy within romantic and marital contexts.

This discussion extends beyond mere economic transactions; it delves into the psychological underpinnings of what individuals seek in relationships. The archetype of the high-value man, as described, not only fulfills a woman's material needs but also caters to her emotional and intellectual desires, thereby assuming a multifaceted role that transcends the traditional provider. This dynamic, while seemingly reinforcing age-old gender stereotypes, also reflects a complex interplay of desires and expectations that shape modern relationships.

Furthermore, the acceptance and practice of polygamy, as hinted at in this context, challenge the conventional monogamous framework, suggesting that financial and emotional security could potentially recalibrate personal boundaries and societal norms. This shift, however, is not without its implications, raising questions about the essence of empowerment, choice, and the true nature of autonomy in romantic engagements.

In dissecting the motivations and outcomes of such relationships, it becomes evident that human connections are woven with threads of tangible and intangible desires. The pursuit of protection, provision, and paternal care, juxtaposed with the willingness to engage in practices like polygamy, underscores a broader quest for fulfillment that defies simple categorization or judgment.

As we navigate these nuanced terrains, the conversation around relationships, resources, and individuals' roles within these constructs invites a deeper reflection on the evolving definitions of partnership, love, and security. It compels us to consider how societal norms and individual aspirations converge and diverge, crafting unique tapestries of human connection that reflect our timeless desires and contemporary complexities.

Women can be hypersexual, too. This type of woman can be challenging if she knows her worth and understands the game. You may just go bankrupt fucking with her.

Long ago, a ship traveled with an English man on board from port to port. At the break of dawn, the ship docked at a port in Italy. The Englishman and the sailors went into town. A young lady caught his eye as the Englishman walked down the street. He asked her if she would join him for a cup of tea. Tea led to breakfast, which led to morning sex that lasted all morning. She put that pussy on him. He had never felt the way she made him feel. He was so pleased that he asked her to go to the masquerade ball, a big event that year. She said yes.

The Mediterranean air was cool, crisp, and still on the night of the ball. The stars were glowing as if they had life. The Englishman took in the night's natural ambiance as he walked to town with thoughts of her flooding his mind with her smell, skin's softness, smile, and hourglass build. He had to control his thoughts, which had begun to morph into thoughts of mounting and dominating her.

Even though everyone wore masks, her curves were unmistakable when she walked into the room; she had consumed his thoughts and her silhouette since their last meeting. There was no denying who she was when she entered the ballroom. She was surprised when he greeted her. While they danced the night away, the other men had expressions as if they knew something that he didn't know. When the clock struck twelve, everyone removed their mask. The lookers began to laugh and point at the Englishman overly. Like the Englishman, they, too, knew her curves and that she was a lady of the night. He had fallen in love with a prostitute. Embarrassed, he became furious and asked the crowd what he should do. The Duke of Dutch went over to the Englishman and told him that this had happened once before in Dutch and that the Dutchmen stripped the woman naked while chanting the word slut. And so they did.

That was the origin of body shaming. The word slut was to lower a woman's self-esteem and take her power away by deterring her from owning their pussy. This still happens today. So, ladies, I want you to take your pussy back and own it. Your beauty and pussy are compelling. History has shown this. Nations have been built and destroyed behind the power you possess when it comes to your pussy.

Some women are for the streets. It's not their fault because they've embraced their sexuality and understand the power of owning their own body. Because of this, they are called whores. Take Lori Harvey's example, who is ranked Queen for holding her body. She is for the streets. She switches up men more than her father switches up suits. Michael B. Jordan never stood a chance. She was never in it for the long haul, just the relationship's honeymoon phase when it was new and exciting. Once that's worn off, it's off to the races again for her. She's like her momma. The difference between the two is that Marjorie does it for the money and fame, and Lori does it for the sport.

Expanding on this, the societal lens often harshly critiques women who freely explore their romantic and sexual options. This narrative taps into the age-old dichotomy of the Madonna-whore complex, where women are pigeonholed into being either pure and untouchable Madonnas or disparaged as whores for their openness and autonomy in their sexual lives. Lori Harvey's navigation through her relationships becomes a larger commentary on society's discomfort with women who refuse to conform to traditional roles of monogamy and subservience, challenging the status quo with their actions.

This discourse isn't just about individual choices but also reflects broader societal anxieties around female autonomy and the fear of the empowered woman. Women like Lori, who own their desires and move through relationships with agency, unsettle the traditional narratives that seek to bind women to a singular path of chastity until marriage, followed by lifelong monogamy. This dynamic is further complicated by the public's fascination and vilification of such women, underscoring a deep-seated cultural ambivalence about female power and autonomy.

Moreover, the juxtaposition of Lori's and Marjorie's motivations—pleasure versus financial gain—opens a window into how women navigate their desires within the constraints of societal judgment. It raises questions about the legitimacy of different motivations for relationship choices and whether the underlying judgments stem from misogyny and the desire to control women's sexuality.

In a world that increasingly champions diversity and freedom of choice, the narrative around women "for the streets" serves as a litmus test for society's progress toward genuinely embracing these values. It confronts the lingering prejudices and double standards that still permeate discussions about gender, sexuality, and relationship dynamics, challenging us to reconsider our attitudes and the language we use to describe women who boldly live their lives on their terms.

Thus, the story of women navigating their romantic lives with agency is not a tale of moral decline but a testament to the ongoing struggle for personal freedom and the redefinition of relationship norms in the face of societal scrutiny. It is a call to embrace complexity over simplicity, understanding over judgment, and autonomy over conformity in the ever-evolving landscape of human relationships.

Lori Harvey's narrative unfolds, mirroring an encounter reminiscent of a personal journey into love's complex labyrinth. Desiring to offer the world to someone only to be met with the modest request for "Texas" is a poignant metaphor for the mismatch of expectations and aspirations that often pervade romantic entanglements. This anecdote underscores the sage advice that attention must be paid when individuals reveal their true selves. The assertion that if someone lacks an essential support system, caution is warranted encapsulates the wisdom of heeding early warnings in relationships.

The portrayal of Lori Harvey and reference to figures like Ciara and Future encapsulates the scrutiny and judgment often cast upon public figures' personal lives, extending the conversation to a broader critique of societal norms surrounding relationships. This discourse delves into the dichotomy of public personas versus private realities, suggesting a deeper examination of what it means to navigate relationships under the watchful eye of societal expectations.

The narrative further expands to include Kendu Isaacs and Kevin Hunter, highlighting that manipulation and expectations are not confined to gender. Their stories, paralleled with the anecdote of addiction's relentless grip, as illustrated by the reference to Pookie's struggle in "New Jack City," serve as allegories for the human condition's complexities. The comparison draws a parallel between the compulsive chase for euphoric highs, whether from substance abuse or the thrill of new relationships, underscoring the cyclical nature of desire and fulfillment.

This expansion critiques the societal penchant for labeling and simplifying complex human behaviors and challenges the reader to consider the multifaceted reasons behind people's actions. It provokes thought on the societal pressures that shape our perceptions of relationships, fidelity, and personal autonomy.

The inclusion of drug use as a metaphor for the insatiable pursuit of pleasure, whether through substances or sexual encounters, invites a reflection on the ways society both condemns and romanticizes the quest for satisfaction. It raises questions about the ethical implications of seeking fulfillment in a world where instant gratification is often valorized at the expense of deeper, more meaningful connections.

An uncle of mine once told me that you can't turn a whore into a housewife until she is tired, and I mean drained. She won't be ready to come to a man's home until her feet get tired of walking. I mean that gravity has taken its toll when her body begins to show signs of age. Only then is it possible to turn a whore into a housewife? You won't have to marry them at this point because they know it's time to settle down. Moving them in and giving them the title of wife is all you must do. No court is needed. She didn't own her agency when she was young.

This stark and unfiltered perspective offers a gritty glimpse into the transactional view of relationships, where her youth and physical allure measure a woman's worth. It's a candid reflection of a mindset deeply ingrained in some parts of society, where women are valued for their sexuality and men for their ability to provide. This viewpoint challenges the notion of mutual respect and partnership in relationships. It underscores a broader societal dilemma about aging, desirability, and the worth of an individual beyond their physical attributes.

By delving into this narrative, we peel back the layers of a complex dialogue about human connections, the commodification of bodies, and the shifting dynamics of relationships as people age. It's a raw examination of how societal and individual perceptions of value, desirability, and power play out in the arena of love and companionship. This conversation is not just about the dichotomy between the so-called "whore" and the housewife but also about challenging and redefining the underlying assumptions that fuel such classifications.

Furthermore, this narrative prompts a deeper inquiry into the nature of fulfillment, satisfaction, and the quest for relationship stability. It raises questions about the criteria we use to judge the readiness for commitment, the societal pressures that shape our views of ideal partnerships, and the personal transformations that lead one to seek a more settled life.

I admire women of the night because they not only know their worth, but they also know their power. They have enough intelligence to put a monetary value on their sexuality. However, they are shamed for this. Why? To strip her of her power. Men are simple and are basically ruled by sex. Women are smart creatures, and most will capitalize on this. Remember, God created Eve because Adam was lonely. Adam was in the garden, engaging with everything that moved. The human male is very sexual. To sexually box him in could be seen as inhumane. It is said that money makes the world go around. Well, that is not entirely true. Sex is what really makes the world go around, and it requires money because of women owning their sexuality. You already know the motto If It Doesn't Make Dollars, Then It Doesn't Make Sense.

Expanding on this, the societal vilification of women who assert control over their sexuality and use it to their advantage is a stark reflection of the broader dynamics of power and control. This discussion sheds light on the double standards embedded within societal norms, where men's sexual freedom is often celebrated or overlooked while women's similar behavior is condemned or stigmatized.

The narrative surrounding women like Lori Harvey, who navigate their relationships with autonomy, becomes a compelling illustration of the clash between traditional expectations and the evolving understanding of female agency. It underscores the tension between societal dictates and individual desires, emphasizing the need to reevaluate how we perceive and value women's choices.

Moreover, the juxtaposition of economic transactions with sexual autonomy invites a deeper examination of the intersections between capitalism, patriarchy, and personal freedom. It challenges us to consider the implications of commodifying sexuality, questioning whether empowerment can truly be achieved within a framework that often exploits and objectifies.

This exploration into the complex interplay of sex, power, and economics not only critiques the societal mechanisms that seek to control and diminish women's power but also celebrates the resilience and ingenuity of those who navigate these treacherous waters. It calls for a more nuanced understanding of sexuality, one that recognizes the inherent worth and agency of individuals, free from the constraints of judgment and moral policing.

In essence, this conversation expansion invites readers to critically engage with the underlying forces that shape our perceptions of sexuality, autonomy, and worth. It encourages a shift towards a more equitable and liberated understanding of human relationships, where the power dynamics of sex and economics are openly acknowledged and navigated with respect and dignity for all individuals involved.

Chapter 7: Dick in Your Hand

Greetings, everyone. Let's get straight to the point. The adage "What's good for the goose is good for the gander," no longer holds up; it's 2024, and it's time to discard outdated mindsets. If you're out here engaging in casual relationships—gracefully, I might add—you must afford your partner, be she your girlfriend, wife, or whatever term you prefer, the same freedoms. If the thought of her with someone else from 10 to 2 doesn't sit well with you, then perhaps you shouldn't be doing it either. Desire to play the field? Then proceed, but remember, even from a young age, we've been subtly encouraged to juggle multiple relationships. Growing up, elders often questioned our romantic statuses, insinuating that having more than one partner was a badge of honor.

We once aspired to explore the ocean's depths and visit the Titanic, a curiosity that, in hindsight, offers little value. As mentioned earlier, it's 2024, and women should have the freedom to explore their desires just as men have, without facing judgment for their choices. Men, it's time to accept this and embrace it. We've lived in a society where double standards were the norm; why not elevate and equalize the playing field?

You've said it yourself: engaging in a casual encounter means nothing to you, so why not grant your partner the same opportunity? There's a saying that if you love something, set it free; if it returns, it's truly yours. Ultimately, isn't that what we all seek? A partner who loves us sincerely and chooses to return to us.

Therefore, I question the societal emphasis on the sanctity of sex. It's an activity we all enjoy, yet we can't be honest with ourselves due to societal norms and unwritten rules. Is it truly correct? We once believed taking a daily aspirin was beneficial, but we learned otherwise years later. Thus, just because society deems something acceptable doesn't necessarily make it so.

We all face choices—good, bad, or indifferent. However, our decisions are primarily driven by societal expectations rather than our feelings. This is particularly true for men. This narrative recounts a period in Tom's life across two different times and the lessons he gleaned. Tom met a woman seventeen years his senior when he was about 21, still figuring out his path in life. Eventually, Tom moved in with her without inquiring about her means of affording a brand-new two-story brick house. At that moment, it seemed irrelevant. Living like a king, with a refrigerator full of food and access to all cable channels, was a luxury. Back then, having cable and watching music videos was a big deal, especially when a Michael Jackson video came on. We used to smoke white paper joints, and she always had skunk weed, which was highly regarded at the time. Life was good—or almost good.

As a real man, having your own money is essential. Relying on someone else's finances is not ideal, regardless of the circumstances. Trust me, no matter how many times you prove your worth, at the end of the day, it's still her money. Soon, she might start giving you an allowance, like $20 a day, making you feel like you're earning minimum wage. As months passed, Tom began to notice odd things. Every Saturday, a lawn man would come to mow the grass without ever collecting payment. Then there was Wednesday. Once a month, Tom was asked to leave the house on Wednesday. At the time, he didn't grasp the significance. All he knew was he had the car and the freedom to be out all day. He would pick up his ex, pretending the new car was his, showcasing his apparent success.

What he didn't realize was how observant women can be. His ex had already gone through the glove box and discovered the car's real owner, whose name was not a woman's. Regarding the Wednesday arrangements, Tom was told a social worker was visiting to assess the woman's attempt to gain custody of her niece's baby. Yet, he never saw the niece or the baby. As time progressed, Tom noticed more peculiarities, like seeing the lawn man at the bank and again at the electric company when they went to pay the bill, always just sitting in his truck, never exiting. Tom couldn't chalk it up to coincidence.

The lawn man was definitely overstepping, and eventually, the situation escalated. Tom discovered that the lawn man was actually a benefactor, taking care of everything for us: the house, car, food, cable – the works. Reflecting on it all, one wonders if things would have been different had she been honest with Tom from the start. Regrettably, there are no second chances, so we'll never know. Considering everything, it's perplexing why Tom was so upset; he should have welcomed the arrangement. He was living his best life: enjoying fine dining, leisurely indulging, and never missing a sporting event on TV. What more could one desire? Yet, Tom couldn't overlook what happened every Wednesday. But it was just one day a month – there were still 30 other days. What harm could possibly be done in one day that couldn't be rectified over the next 30? And yet, Tom lamented over this single day. Any discomfort would be temporary, easily soothed with some ice, and she'd recover in no time. Meanwhile, there were other ways to be satisfied.

What Tom failed to realize was that his pride was clouding his judgment. Pride is peculiar; it can compel you to uphold your principles and lead to irrational decisions. Angry and wounded by pride, he left, forfeiting the financial security and the comforts he had. And for what? He wastes years of his life, moving back into his mother's house and starting from scratch – all because of pride. Now, he's back home, jobless and broke, consuming his mother's limited resources. He even overhears his mother telling her friends about his return, lamenting how his presence means she can't entertain her own company. It's a stark reminder of the consequences of letting pride dictate your actions, especially when nothing has changed except his circumstances, now relegated to his old room, a tangible symbol of his choices.

In this second story, I will share that Tom, much older now, has made something of his life. He became a project manager for an air conditioning company. After experiencing life and a couple of divorces, Tom decided to pursue a different type of woman. From Tom's perspective, having aged and gained experience, he values real-world lessons over theoretical knowledge. He believes that experience is the best teacher. You might read every book available, but you truly learn through experiencing life firsthand. I can't tell you how many times someone with a college degree has come out to the field only to find themselves completely lost, exclaiming, "It didn't look like this in the classroom."

Tom's first wife was a nurse practitioner, and his second wife was a marketing director. Thus, Tom was searching for someone fundamentally different this time—someone less academically inclined, a "plain Jane" where education wasn't a priority. Eventually, Tom met a younger woman, fifteen years his junior, who had two daughters. Tom had never encountered a woman like her before—she was from a challenging background, a real "ghetto girl." This relationship was thrilling for Tom, at least initially. It's always intriguing to encounter something new, but paying attention is crucial. There's a difference between what someone says and what they show you about themselves. She once told Tom that she doubted she had enough people to carry her to the grave—a statement that should have been a glaring warning sign for Tom.

However, hindsight is always 20/20. As the relationship progressed, Tom began noticing concerning behaviors. For instance, during a trip to Walmart, they picked up a few items and headed to the self-checkout lane. Now, accidentally missing scanning an item or two is understandable, but deliberately not scanning every other item is something Tom couldn't condone. The idea of facing legal consequences over a pack of wings and a pound cake, despite having enough money to pay for them, was absurd to him. Furthermore, Tom noticed that wherever they went, the outing turned into a hustle, which he could not support or condone.

So, one must ask oneself: is it hustling or haggling? The third thing Tom noticed was that whenever they went out to get food, she always ordered two entrées, claiming they were for her girls. Taking care of one's children is commendable, but the problem was that the girls never received the food. You might think she was giving it to someone else, but as it turns out, it was for her to eat the next day. She was simply being greedy. However, her hustling eventually caught up with her, and she was arrested on serious charges. After weeks of calls and pleading, Tom, against his better judgment, bailed her out of jail.

In the following months, Tom realized he was unwilling to assist her with her legal troubles. He said, "It's your mess; you fix it." Then, it was discovered she had more charges for other crimes she had committed. Tom urged her to find a job and address her issues. Instead, she found a sugar daddy, leaving Tom again frustrated and distancing himself from the situation. Why be upset over something you were unwilling to do? Not only did the sugar daddy cover her legal fees, but he also bought her a car, clothes, and a new apartment—all things Tom was unwilling to provide.

Tom learned nothing from his past experiences and continued to let his pride dominate. In a story that Tom could have shared with his friends and perhaps found happiness, he once again finds himself alone at home, consumed by his pride.

Food is good for the body, but remember, you are what you eat. Cutting back on fast food is essential. The advice to avoid McDonald's, Burger King, and Wendy's and opt for single meat and small fries if fast food is a must underscores a broader narrative about health and well-being. This guidance highlights the negative impact of processed foods on physical health and subtly hints at the social and intimate implications of dietary choices. The suggestion that one's diet can influence personal relationships and desirability touches on a rarely discussed aspect of health and wellness.

The mention of Dr. Sebi and the alkaline diet introduces an alternative perspective on nutrition, emphasizing the potential for diet to enhance energy levels and improve overall health, including sexual health. This approach to nutrition and its connection to vitality and well-being invites readers to reconsider the conventional wisdom surrounding diet and lifestyle.

Moreover, the encouragement towards exercise, with the adage from the author's grandfather to "Get up and do something, even if it's wrong," serves as a motivational call to action. It speaks to the importance of physical activity for health and as a fundamental aspect of living fully. The incremental approach to exercise, suggesting starting with what one can do and gradually increasing the effort, offers a practical and inclusive strategy for enhancing physical fitness and, by extension, quality of life.

This discussion about diet and exercise transcends the physical, touching on life's intimate and personal dimensions. It challenges readers to consider how their lifestyle choices impact their health, relationships, and sexual satisfaction. The emphasis on personal responsibility and incremental improvement reflects a broader theme of empowerment and self-determination, encouraging individuals to take control of their health and, by extension, their happiness.

Now I have some tips I will share with you guys and gals. Guys up first. I can help you with almost anything, but if you have a small penis (Vienna sausage), you only have two choices. Kill yourself or have surgery. If surgery doesn't work, you always have first choice.

If you have Erectile dysfunction, known as ED, here are a few tips to get you up and going. Sixty percent of 60% of men haven't seen below because they have an ED problem. It's in your gut. Lose your gut, lose your ED problem. At one time, I was out here looking nine months pregnant. People asked me if I was a rapper whenever I went to Houston. What is it with Houston rappers and beer bellies? As soon as I lost that gut, I found three inches of my penis, and people stopped confusing me for a Houston rapper.

It was nice to be able to look down and see some penis. The more your gut sticks out, the more your penis goes inside your fat. Fruit and seeds are the key. They taste good and are good for the body. Strawberries are the best. Eat three strawberries and four almonds daily for a month; you will notice a big difference. Try a stick of ginseng. Just chew on it all day, and you will feel its effects all over your body, especially downstairs. Sea moss and goat weed are good natural remedies, too. An old-school player told me he's never had any dick issues because he takes a spoonful of honey every day.

Viagra has been on the market for decades and has been taken by hundreds of thousands of men. Like all medicines, it has side effects. Sometimes, it works; sometimes, it works too well. After many men reported prolonged hard-ons, young men began taking the drug so that that could stay in a young woman's pussy for hours. Medicines have a way of not working after a certain period. The body will eventually become immune by building up a tolerance for the medication. It no longer has the effects it once had on the body, much like monogamous sex.

Another option you may want to consider is the penis shot which is an injection at the base of your penis. I tried it. Not going to say why I tried it, but I can say peer pressure is a mother fucker. The shot had my penis on hard for six hours. I fucked a woman for five hours straight. I poured the meat into her backside all night, giving her the dick. The next day, she didn't say anything the entire drive to her home.

When I tried to engage her in conversation, she only nodded. While holding the steering wheel in my left hand, I gently caressed her thigh with my right hand. Nothing too long. In that quick touch, I felt her trembling, which caused me to pull my hand back. As we approached her home, she jumped out of the car before I could pull into the driveway. That was the last time I saw her. I heard she became a lesbian. That's the second time I have driven a girl from straight to lesbian.

One of my favorite natural remedies for a strong hard-on is rubber band therapy. You will need a rubber band, a small bowl, and ice to fill the bowl. Have you ever been in a Cryo chamber? It's the same concept, but it will just be your nuts instead of rejuvenating your whole body.

First, tie the rubber band around the base of your penis and nut sack. You want the rubber band snug but not too tight. Then, fill the bowl with ice. Sit your nuts in an ice bowl for 15 minutes. Do this once a week. Wow, that is all I can say. It will make you feel as if you are twenty-seven years old. Your penis will be so hard.

Now for women, if your vagina is broken down there, there is nothing that can be done but practice your oral sex. Make it so good that he will forget about pussy. It will be hard as hell, but it can be done. The only problem you may have is that you can end up with dick-sucking lips. This is when you have wrinkles around your upper and lower lips. A remedy is to get some oatmeal, baking powder, and toothpaste, then mix it all. Apply it to your lips and leave it on for 15 minutes before rinsing off. Do this three times a week; it will knock those wrinkles right on out and keep them at bay.

Now, if you have an odor down there or your man has told you that you smell like salmon croquette down there, go to a doctor to see what is causing the foul smell.

I once dated a girl who was a herbalist, and she would routinely turn her vagina into a fruit salad. You would think it was for my enjoyment, but it wasn't. It seems she believed this was a natural remedy to control vagina odor.

This pussy odor control concoction would consist of fresh-cut strawberries that were rolled in corn and then placed inside her vagina. Then she would take a banana and place it on top of her vagina. Nestled in the folds just on top of her vulva. She literally and figuratively turned her vagina would be a fruit bowl for 15 minutes three times a week, every week.

Washing your vagina in baking soda has been a natural pussy odor control since baking soda was invented. It absorbs all odors.

If you don't have a snapper or your vagina has become a little worn out from you not owning your pussy. Your elasticity has left your vagina walls, leaving it loosey-goosey, and you can't seem to tighten it up. You may want to try the Yoni egg that you place inside your vagina cavity and hold for as long as you can. Then you'd repeat it just as you would any other exercise. By doing this, you are strengthening your vagina walls as well as learning to contract them. Snapper pussy.

Bathing in vinegar has been known to tighten up your pussy as well. But this should only be done once a week if you don't want pickled pussy.

In Dr. Cock and Balls' insightful narrative within "Shenigga's," Chapter Five delves into the Amazon Warriors, unveiling a matriarchal society where women not only thrived in roles typically dominated by men but also redefined the essence of power and autonomy. This society, where women were the supreme leaders, and men played subservient roles, epitomizes the historical concept of "owning your pussy" — a phrase symbolizing women's complete control over their bodies and choices, a stark contrast to the patriarchal norms prevalent in other civilizations.

Dr. Cock and Balls meticulously categorize the women of the Amazon, illustrating a society rich in diversity and functionality. From agriculturists nurturing the land to hunters venturing into the wilderness for sustenance and homemakers ensuring the continuity of daily life, each woman played a pivotal role in sustaining their society's well-being. Among these, the militia stood out — female warriors embodying strength and strategy, capturing men not as partners but as means for procreation and labor, a radical inversion of traditional gender roles.

The ritualistic approach to procreation, devoid of sexual contact with male captives, underscores the Amazons' pursuit of physical and mental autonomy, viewing men as potential threats to their strength and coherence. The use of the Uaqui fruit, leading to temporary genital closure, is perhaps the most striking testament to their commitment to celibacy and independence, a physical manifestation of their societal ideals and a barrier against any form of external control.

Furthermore, the preference for female offspring and the systematic exclusion of male progeny highlight a deliberate effort to perpetuate matriarchal lineage, ensuring the community's sustainability without compromising its foundational principles. While seemingly harsh, this approach reflects a nuanced understanding of their environment and the necessities dictated by their societal structure.

The extract of the South American fruit, costing fifty dollars per ounce, is touted as a miraculous rejuvenator for those seeking to restore their intimacy to a state of perceived virginity. This narrative, steeped in the search for eternal youth and vitality, speaks to a deeper societal obsession with purity and restoring what has been lost or diminished over time. The suggestion to continue sexual activity during the treatment as a means to gauge effectiveness adds a layer of practicality to the magical, almost alchemical promise of transformation.

This pursuit of rejuvenation, while seemingly a simple solution to complex issues of self-esteem and bodily autonomy, opens a broader discussion on the commodification of women's bodies and the pressures to conform to idealized standards of sexual desirability. It reflects a society where the value of a woman is often tied to her sexual appeal and perceived purity, echoing age-old narratives that prize virginity and youth above experience and individuality.

Moreover, the warning of potential chafing and dryness as side effects underscores the physical risks women are encouraged to take to meet these standards. The recommendation to have lubricant on standby not only speaks to the practical considerations of engaging in sexual activity but also metaphorically highlights the friction between societal expectations and the reality of women's lived experiences.

This discussion extends beyond the physical realm, touching on the psychological impact of striving for an unattainable ideal. It challenges readers to consider the lengths to which society pushes individuals to alter themselves in pursuit of acceptance and love, often at the expense of their well-being and autonomy. The narrative is a provocative critique of how commercial solutions prey on insecurities, promising empowerment through conformity to a commercialized, commodified ideal of sexual purity.

For you who experience insomnia, which is literally in your head. See Dr. Pussisotite explains in her book *Two Dicks Upside the Head* that after ladies sit on her pussy and not having sex, the brain stops sending out secretions, hormones in a woman's body that act like a natural sleep aid. Dr. Pussisotite explains that having sex and keeping our hormones in balance is a lot better than taking medicine. After a while, your body builds up a tolerance to sleep medicine or alcohol. Drinking wine every day makes you want more and more. Next thing you know, you have alcoholism. That's not good for anybody. Masturbation is the remedy, and it's also empowering and liberating.

Medical

To be considered an expert in the nuanced world of intimacy, one must possess an in-depth understanding of the vagina, recognizing its variations across different body types. This understanding is crucial, as the physical characteristics of women significantly influence the positioning of the vagina, affecting intimate interactions. The categorization based on body type — from slender to thick, each with its unique anatomical positioning — underscores the necessity of a tailored approach to intimacy, respecting and celebrating the diversity of women's bodies.

Acknowledging these differences is more than an anatomical observation; it invites exploring the art of pleasure with mindfulness and adaptability. It suggests that engaging intimately with a partner goes beyond mere physicality, requiring an appreciation for the uniqueness of each individual's body and openness to adapt one's approach accordingly.

Rudy Ray Moore's philosophy that "Sex is an art. Give it your all" resonates deeply within this context, serving as a guiding principle for those committed to enriching their monogamous relationships. This approach encourages partners to invest themselves fully in their sexual expression, exploring and expanding their boundaries to maintain a vibrant and fulfilling sexual connection. It's a call to approach intimacy with creativity, enthusiasm, and a willingness to discover and rediscover one another's desires and pleasures continually.

The advice to remain engaged and exploratory in one's sex life, even within the framework of monogamy, challenges the misconception that long-term relationships inevitably lead to a decline in sexual excitement. Instead, it posits that with effort, communication, and a spirit of adventure, couples can sustain and even deepen their sexual connection over time.

While maintaining a direct and somewhat provocative tone, this narrative emphasizes the importance of understanding, respect, and communication in navigating the complexities of intimate relationships. It advocates for a conscious effort to keep the spark alive, urging couples to view their sexual journey as an ongoing adventure marked by mutual exploration, understanding, and growth.

The Coital Alignment Technique (CAT) enhances the intimacy of the traditional missionary position through a deliberate alignment that prioritizes clitoral stimulation. This technique, involving partners lying face to face with the penetrating partner on top, sliding to create friction against the clitoris before penetration, intensifies the physical connection between partners. The emphasis on pressure and friction augments the sensory experience and fosters a deeper emotional bond through heightened face-to-face intimacy.

By virtue of its design to maximize physical contact and stimulation, this thoughtful engagement in CAT serves as a pathway to enhanced pleasure and a testament to the multifaceted benefits of intimate physical activities. It represents a confluence of emotional connection and physical health, highlighting the importance of understanding and exploring the dynamics of one's sexual relationships within overall wellness.

Burns __140__ calories in 30 minutes.

The Countertop Position – My second-best position- is revered for its unique blend of depth, control, and intimacy and stands as a testament to the exploratory nature of human sexuality. This position, often likened to a frontal variation of the universally cherished doggy style, offers a fresh perspective on traditional intimacy, blending physical depth with emotional closeness. Having the receiving partner positioned akin to a visit to the gynecologist sets the stage for a deeply penetrative experience that transcends the mere physicality of the act.

The essence of this position lies in the penetrator's ability to harness control over depth and speed, making it a dance of synchronicity and mutual satisfaction. The pivotal role of hand placement on the hips provides stability and acts as a conduit for conveying desires and rhythm without words. This deliberate hand placement allows for a meticulous exploration of pleasure, emphasizing the importance of non-verbal communication in sexual encounters.

Moreover, the Countertop position uniquely accommodates the receiver's autonomy in pleasure, granting them the liberty to engage in self-stimulation. This act of masturbation during intercourse is not just a pathway to enhanced pleasure but also a bold statement on the significance of self-awareness and agency in one's sexual experiences. It reinforces the narrative that mutual satisfaction is paramount and that pleasure is a shared journey rather than a solitary quest.

Burns 85 - 100   calories in 30 minutes.

Clitoral Stimulation- given its profound impact on overcoming orgasmic challenges, underscores the intricate dance of pleasure and satisfaction in sexual encounters. With the clitoris harboring 8,000 nerve endings, its stimulation presents a potent avenue for enhancing the receiver's climax. This method, employing a blend of flicks, swirls, and gentle sucks, is not just a technique but an art form deeply rooted in the understanding and appreciation of the partner's body. This approach addresses the physical aspect of pleasure and nurtures an emotional connection, affirming the partner's needs and desires.

Burns __85 - 100__ calories in 30 minutes.

The **Rocking Horse** position is a testament to the art of intimate connection, emphasizing G-spot stimulation through a synchronized, rocking motion. This face-to-face configuration allows both partners to engage deeply, with the penetrator's arms cuffed beneath the receiver's legs, enhancing both the emotional and physical intensity of the encounter. It's a dance of depth and speed control, offering a shared journey towards mutual climax. This position does not just stimulate physically but also strengthens the bond between partners, making every moment an exploration of each other's desires and responses.

On the other hand, **Seated Scissors** merges visual appeal with clitoral stimulation, crafting a scenario that tantalizes both partners. The receiver, straddling the penetrator backward, finds rhythm against the leg that acts as a 'grinding board,' ensuring pleasure is both seen and felt. This position, ideal for those who relish visual stimuli, offers a panoramic view of the body's movements, accentuating the sensual ripples and curves. It's a celebration of form and sensation, where each thrust and grind resonates with an energetic melody of bodies in sync.

Burns 85 - 100   calories in 30 minutes.

The **Hands Behind Ankles** position offers a nuanced approach to intimacy, emphasizing physical closeness and the exploration of new sensations. By laying the partner on her stomach and adopting a 45-degree angle for penetration, this position facilitates a deeper connection, both physically and emotionally. The act of the receiving partner grabbing her ankles, optionally secured with toy cuffs for those who enjoy an element of bondage, introduces an element of trust and vulnerability into the encounter. This position, while enhancing the sensation of tightness, also opens up a space for couples to explore their boundaries and desires in a safe, consensual environment. The recommendation of a safe word underscores the importance of communication and mutual respect, making the experience not just about physical pleasure but also about deepening the couple's bond through shared exploration and understanding.

Burns 85 - 100   calories burnt in 30 minutes.

Speaking of safe words, **Asphyxiation** has been known to cause stimulation. This is when the penetrator simulates strangulation while penetrating the receiver without killing her. A safe word is definitely needed when practiced.

Burns 85-100   calories burnt in 30 minutes.

Incorporating fruit into your sexual activities can add an element of fun and experimentation, offering a playful twist to intimacy. However, it's crucial to pay attention to how your body reacts. If you find the juice from fruits causing an uncomfortable tingling sensation in your vagina, it's a clear sign that something's amiss. This discomfort is your body's way of signaling that your vaginal health might be compromised, prompting a necessary consultation with a healthcare provider.

To add 2 inches to your manhood, start by tying a string around the tip of your penis, letting it dangle a full foot downward. Attach a tennis ball to the other end of the string. This might sound unusual, but just like any other muscle in your body, your penis will grow with regular exercise. Perform four sets of 25 repetitions three times a week. You'll be surprised at how effective this simple method can be.

If you're struggling to achieve rock-hard erections, it's time to put aside the pills and creams and try a more natural approach. Place a bag of ice under your scrotum for 15 minutes thrice a week. This method might remind you of a cryo-chamber, which rejuvenates your body by exposing it to extreme cold. However, this technique focuses on just your testicles. Believe me, you will notice a significant difference after a month of consistent practice.

And don't forget about the importance of regular masturbation. Masturbating is beneficial, even if you're married or have a girlfriend. It helps keep your "pipes" free from debris. Remember, your penis is a muscle—regular workouts will keep it in shape. So, the more you engage, the better. A vibrant and exhilarating sex life holds equal weight to maintaining one that's physically sound. Yogurt, for instance, has gained recognition for its beneficial effects in sustaining a balanced vaginal pH level, a crucial aspect of feminine health. This piece of advice comes in handy, particularly if the unconventional use of food items, like bread shaped as sex toys, leads to unexpected infections such as yeast infections. Such scenarios underline the importance of being mindful about introducing edible items into your sexual encounters, ensuring they contribute positively to both pleasure and well-being.

Maintaining a balance between enjoyment and health in your sexual experiences is not just advisable; it's essential. The use of fruits and other food items should enhance your intimacy, not compromise it. Always listen to your body's responses and prioritize your health by seeking professional advice when things feel off. Remember, an adventurous sex life is a healthy one as long as it's approached with awareness and care.

Chapter 8: Conclusion

My great grandpa, a man of few words but profound wisdom, had this peculiar pocket watch that caught my attention one lazy Saturday morning. He was gearing up for his usual trip into town and asked me to fetch the watch from its resting place on the nightstand as if it were a test of my reliability. Eager to please, I scampered off, my little legs carrying me faster than my excitement.

When I found it, that unmistakable pull of curiosity had me cracking open the watch, expecting to see the familiar hands and numbers. Instead, I was met with my reflection staring back at me from a mirror where the clock should have been.

Baffled, I brought the watch, or the mirror, to my great-grandpa, my young mind buzzing with questions. Why would anyone replace a perfect clock with a mirror? It seemed like the kind of practical joke life was too busy to play. When I posed the question to him, his eyes twinkled with the sort of secret that adults hoard like treasures.

"Son," he said, his voice carrying the weight of unspoken stories, "you can lie to the whole world, but you cannot lie to yourself."

This was no ordinary mirror; it was a tool for introspection, a guardian of truth in a world too cluttered with falsehoods.

This watch mirror wasn't about telling time; it was about understanding time's value, about recognizing the moments that demand honesty above all. Before making any decision, Grandpa would pull out that watch, not to check the hour, but to confront his reflection, to ensure his actions aligned with his core. It was a ritual of self-accountability, a private moment where one could not hide from the truth.

In a world where truth often plays hide and seek, where decisions are cloaked in layers of justification, this lesson from my great-grandpa stands as a beacon. It's easy to get lost in the sea of expectations, to wear masks so long we forget the face beneath. The mirror in that watch served as a reminder that the most crucial approval comes not from the crowd but from the person in the reflection.

To this day, I carry the essence of that lesson with me. It's not about the literal mirror or even the act of looking into it; it's about cultivating a practice of self-reflection, of pausing in our relentless pursuit of the next big thing to ensure we're not losing ourselves in the process. In a society that often prioritizes appearance over authenticity, remembering my great-grandpa's mirror watch is a call to embrace honesty, starting with the person we face in the mirror each day.If you've ever been labeled as angry, mad, hostile, or bitter, take a moment to reflect on these words. They might sting, but they could also shed light on truths you must face before diving into the deep end of a monogamous relationship. Jumping into such a commitment without addressing the emotional baggage you're lugging around is akin to setting yourself and your potential partner up for a spectacular nosedive into disappointment.

Let's cut straight to the chase: unresolved issues, especially those festering wounds left by past relationships, are like time bombs in your emotional luggage. They tick away silently until one day, they explode, splattering bits of resentment and dissatisfaction over your current love life. It's not about blaming exes or dwelling on what went wrong. No, this is about introspection, about taking a hard look in the mirror and acknowledging the scars you've carried forward.

Carrying these unresolved issues into a new relationship is a surefire way to sabotage it. Imagine trying to build a house on quicksand; no matter how beautiful the blueprint, it will sink. That happens when you drag unresolved anger and bitterness into a new relationship. You might think you're hiding it well, but these feelings can seep out, poisoning the well of love you're trying to drink from.

This isn't about indulging in self-pity or wallowing in what-ifs. It's about taking control, about deciding you won't be the architect of your unhappiness any longer. It's about being honest with yourself and recognizing that healing is a prerequisite to happiness, not a byproduct of finding someone new. Before you can truly commit to someone else, you must commit to yourself—to healing, to growth, and to shed those layers of bitterness that have clung to you like a second skin.

Let's face it: the shopping list for a permanent mate can sometimes read like a fantasy draft in a league where reality doesn't qualify. Women, on the one hand, are often believed to be scouting for that tall, dark, and handsome fellow whose bank account is as robust as his physique, cruising around in a high-end car, dwelling in a mansion, and somehow, miraculously, perfectly balanced on the masculine-feminine spectrum. Then there are the men, supposedly on the hunt for a goddess who's mastered the art of eternal beauty, juggles culinary genius with a career, moonlights as a supermodel, and embodies the paradox of being a saint in the streets and a siren in the sheets, all while maintaining the emotional fortitude of a Zen master.

Consider this riddle: a person can be locked up for ten years, and as soon as he gets out, he runs straight to a crack house. Despite not having had it in 10 years, something drives him there, reminiscent of Pookie in "New Jack City," saying, "Man, these streets keep calling me."

Similarly, consider Papa Murphy's business model, where they make your pizza and charge full price, but you take it home and cook it yourself. Like what?

What if I'm hungry and want to eat a slice on the way home?

Lastly, DJ Khaled is another enigma; he never raps a verse or spits a bar, yet he keeps having number-one albums by just saying, "Another one."

Men generally seek a firm and fit body, a woman with hair, a good personality, and education—though the latter is not a must, it is undoubtedly a plus. However, they often end up with gold diggers, even if the woman has her own money.

On the other hand, women are looking for men who are in touch with their feminine side, not afraid to cry or show emotion, and who help with hair and nails. Ladies, you may already have that in your best gay friend, Tyrone. So, you have a decision to make: do you want your gay friend or a real man?

This caricature of expectations is not just unrealistic; it's a recipe for disappointment dressed as ambition. These laundry lists of ideal partner traits don't just set the bar high; they launch it into a different stratosphere, leaving little room for the beautifully flawed human reality. What's often left unsaid in this pursuit of perfection is acknowledging our imperfections and understanding that relationships are not transactions. They're about connection, compromise, and the mutual growth that comes from navigating life's unpredictable waters together.

The problem with these societal blueprints is that they ignore the essence of human connection. At their core, relationships are about finding someone whose company you enjoy, who challenges you, supports you, and grows with you. It's about finding joy in the little things, like shared laughter over a home-cooked meal (which, by the way, can be a joint venture) or the comfort of silence when words are unnecessary. It's about recognizing that beauty fades, bank accounts fluctuate, and bodies change, but the qualities that truly matter—kindness, respect, humor, and loyalty—stand the test of time.

Embarking on a journey of self-improvement and partnership enhancement starts with a candid look in the mirror. Before you dive headlong into the dating pool or attempt to fix what might seem broken in your love life, pause. Assess the emotional bruises and scars from past relationships. It's crucial to acknowledge that we often orbit around a specific type of individual, a pattern that, despite our best intentions, tends to lead us down familiar paths of disappointment. The stark truth? More often than not, the common thread in these repeated narratives is us.

This realization isn't meant to be a harsh critique but a call to introspection. Understand what you desire in a partner and what you're prepared to contribute to the relationship. A 90-day rule could be a pragmatic approach, allowing time to evaluate the mutual investment in the budding relationship.

But let's get honest about the quest for the 'perfect mate.' If you're holding out for a flawless partner, you're setting yourself up for an endless wait. Instead, embrace the potential to 'build' your mate, not from a place of superficiality but from genuine mutual growth. Yes, your partner should bring something to the table—nobody's looking to craft a partner from thin air, akin to a Build-a-Bear workshop. Yet, the foundation of a strong relationship often lies in supporting each other's dreams and aspirations.

For instance, discover their passions and talents if your partner's career is in limbo. Maybe crafting a resume or exploring educational opportunities could be your joint project. And if it's something as tangible as dental work that's needed, exploring options together—from insurance to government assistance—can strengthen bonds and show commitment.

However, tread carefully with the notion of 'building' your partner. The dynamic of transformation within a relationship is complex. While some argue that a man who invests in a woman's growth secures loyalty, others suggest that a woman doing the same might inadvertently prepare her partner to explore new horizons. This perspective, though controversial, highlights the unpredictable nature of human relationships and the sexual dynamics often attributed to men.

Challenging these stereotypes requires a nuanced understanding of partnership. It's not about molding someone into an ideal but fostering an environment where both partners can grow, learn, and evolve together. This journey of mutual enhancement should be rooted in respect, understanding, and a genuine desire for each other's happiness, transcending traditional narratives of dependency and transformation.

Let's get one thing straight, folks—dragging your old relationship drama into your new romance is like trying to start a new painting on a canvas already used for a failed art project. You're just setting yourself up for a mess. Picture this: you're having a chill night, everything's going smoothly, and then boom, your partner leaves the toilet seat up. Suddenly, it's not just a minor inconvenience; it's World War III in your bathroom. But here's the kicker: it's not about the seat or the clothes left outside the gym bag—it's about the ghost of exes past lurking in your present.

Dr. Tas Tnutt, in his groundbreaking book "The New 90-Day Rule," hits the nail on the head. He suggests a detox period of 90 days post-breakup if you've been in a year-long relationship. For every year you've been entangled in love's web, tack on another 90 days to clear the emotional clutter. It's about giving yourself the space to breathe, to purge the lingering essence of your ex from your system.

And let's not skirt around the bush—Dr. Tas Tnutt also dives into the exploration phase, where you're encouraged to meet a parade of Mr. Wrongs while looking for Mr. Right. It's a journey of discovery, of figuring out what ticks your boxes, from the tall ones to the short ones, the buff ones to the lean ones. It's an expedition to understand your desires and what you seek in a partner.

Then there's the twist—your ideal man might be your best friend, Kevin. But plot twist: Kevin's on his quest, possibly searching for the same thing you are. The narrative here isn't just about finding love or lust; it's about self-discovery, understanding your wants and needs, and realizing that sometimes, what we're searching for in a partner might already be present in the friendships we hold dear.

So, before jumping into a new romantic venture, ensure you're not carrying old baggage. Unpack and declutter, and then, only then, are you truly ready to paint a new masterpiece on a clean canvas.

We can all agree that both men and women seek love. However, with love often comes lust, and while lust may diminish over time, love can still remain, though perhaps not as intense as it once was. The heart wants what it wants. That's why, when you see certain couples, your first thought might be that she is with him for his money or that a larger woman with a smaller man financially supports him. However, that's not always the case. As mentioned earlier, love is strange, and the workings of the mind are stranger.

In the grand scheme of things, challenging norms is not just liberating; it's necessary. It's about dismantling the fantasy to reveal the beauty of reality. It's about understanding that a partner is not an accessory to your life but a co-navigator on a journey filled with highs, lows, and the mundane in-betweens. By shifting the focus from what society says we should want to what we truly need, we open ourselves up to the possibilities of genuine, deep connections not predicated on superficial benchmarks but on love's real, messy, and wonderful essence.

More often than not, finding the perfect partner feels like chasing a mirage in the desert of human relationships. I have attempted to dismantle our elaborate fantasies, revealing the raw truth beneath the layers of societal pressure and personal longing. The conclusion drawn is not just a call for introspection but a manifesto for redefining our approach to love and partnership.

In this journey of self-discovery and mutual growth, I urge readers to strip away the veneer of superficiality and embrace the flawed beauty of human connection. We must confront our past baggage, to detoxify our emotional landscape before embarking on new romantic adventures. Dr. Tas Tnutt's innovative approach, advocating for a period of emotional cleansing post-breakup, resonates as a beacon of wisdom in a sea of relationship advice.

Moreover, I invite you to explore the fluidity of desire and the unpredictability of attraction, challenge stereotypes and norms, to seek fulfillment not in the checkboxes of societal expectations but in the genuine connection forged between two souls navigating the complexities of life together.

As I close the pages of "Monogamy is a Myth," we are left with a profound realization: love is not a destination but a journey marked by shared laughter, silent understanding, and unwavering support. It's about finding joy in the mundane and strength in vulnerability. By embracing the messiness of reality, we pave the way for authentic, enduring connections that transcend the constraints of societal constructs. Let's not forget that true love isn't found in pursuing perfection but in accepting imperfection—in embracing the beautifully flawed essence of what it means to be human.